SO YOU THINK YOU KNOW ALEX RIDER

*Hodder
Children's
Books*

A division of Hodder Headline Limited

© Copyright Hodder Children's Books 2006

Published in Great Britain in 2006
by Hodder Children's Books

Editor: Isabel Thurston
Design by Fiona Webb
Cover design: Hodder Children's Books

The right of Clive Gifford to be identified as the author
of the work has been asserted by him in accordance
with the Copyright, Designs and Patents Act 1988.

10 9 8 7 6 5 4 3 2

ISBN-10: 0340 91713 X
ISBN-13: 978 0 340 91713 8

Printed by Bookmarque Ltd, Croydon, Surrey

The paper and board used in this paperback by
Hodder Children's Books are natural recyclable products
made from wood grown in sustainable forests. The
manufacturing processes conform to the environmental
regulations of the country of origin.

Hodder Children's Books
a division of Hodder Headline Limited
338 Euston Road
London NW1 3BH

CONTENTS

Introduction

Questions

INTRODUCTION

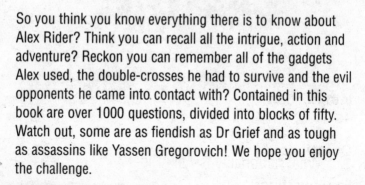

So you think you know everything there is to know about Alex Rider? Think you can recall all the intrigue, action and adventure? Reckon you can remember all of the gadgets Alex used, the double-crosses he had to survive and the evil opponents he came into contact with? Contained in this book are over 1000 questions, divided into blocks of fifty. Watch out, some are as fiendish as Dr Grief and as tough as assassins like Yassen Gregorovich! We hope you enjoy the challenge.

ABOUT THE AUTHOR

Clive Gifford is an award-winning author of more than eighty books for children and adults including *Espionage and Disinformation*, *Spies* and *Space Facts and Records*. He is the author of Hodder Children's Books' *So You Think You Know?* series of quiz books including titles on *The Simpsons*, *The Lord of the Rings*, *Roald Dahl*, *Premier League Football* and *Dr Who*. Clive can be contacted at his website: www.clivegifford.co.uk.

EASY QUESTIONS

1. What nationality is Alex Rider?

2. What was the name of Alex Rider's uncle, with whom he used to live?

3. What martial art is Alex very good at?

4. What was a Stormbreaker: a satellite, a computer or a helicopter?

5. What was the name of the MI6 staff member who produced a range of gadgets for Alex?

6. For which agency do Alan Blunt, Mrs Jones and John Crawley all work: SAS, MI5, MI6 or SBS?

7. In which city does Alex Rider live?

8. What was the first name of Alex's best school friend in the book *Scorpia*: Tim, Tam or Tom?

9. Was Consanto Enterprises based in Italy, Spain or France?

10. Is the first book in the Alex Rider series
    Eagle Strike, *Point Blanc* or *Stormbreaker*?

11. Who was Alex sent to kill by Scorpia?

12. In which book did Alex Rider head into space?

13. What flavour was the bubblegum that
    Smithers gave Alex?

14. When Alex rode a snowboard did he adopt a
    regular or goofy stance?

15. In the second book, what is the name of the
    academy for troublesome rich boys that Alex
    is sent to?

16. In *Skeleton Key*, what job does Alex do at
    Wimbledon?

17. What was the name of the first hotel in
    space?

18. At the start of the series, who had come to
    London seven years ago and had become one
    of Alex's closest friends?

19. Whose plane is known as Air Force One?

20. In *Eagle Strike*, which evil opponent of Alex's
    was a famous pop star and vegetarian?

21. Who was the first person chosen to play the Gameslayer computer at its launch?

22. In which book did Yassen Gregorovich die: *Stormbreaker*, *Scorpia* or *Eagle Strike*?

23. Was Alex to fight the first, third or nineteenth bull in the bullfight in *Eagle Strike*?

24. In which book did a Russian general want to adopt Alex Rider?

25. What is the name of the bald, very fat MI6 member with a moustache Alex first met in *Stormbreaker*?

26. Was an Ocean Beach Thruster: a jet ski, a surfboard, or a speedboat?

27. Did Drevin say that his second, smaller, rocket was to carry: an ape, a dog or some mice for a space experiment?

28. In which book was Alex attacked by a Siberian tiger?

29. What was the first name of the girl Alex became great friends with at Wimbledon: Sandra, Sam or Sabina?

30. After Ian Rider died, who became Alex Rider's legal guardian: Alan Blunt, Edward Pleasure or Jack Starbright?

31. What was the name of the Russian billionaire in *Ark Angel*?

32. Boris Kiriyenko was the president of which country?

33. What does SAS stand for?

34. Who did Ian Rider leave his house and all his money to?

35. In *Scorpia*, who threw a Samurai sword at Alex, trying to kill him: Mrs Rothman or Nile?

36. Is the prologue to *Eagle Strike* set in the Malayan, Amazon or African jungle?

37. Which woman in *Point Blanc* smoked cigars?

38. What part of Skoda's body suffered a broken bone as the barge was lifted into the air?

39. What was the name of the man whose face was disfigured after a knife-throwing accident?

40. In what country was Yassen Gregorovich born: Russia, Estonia or Poland?

41. In which Alex Rider book does Alex first work with members of the CIA?

42. Is Jack Starbright's title Dr, Mr, Mrs or Miss?

43. What creature was the sign of Scorpia?

44. In what English city was Alex held prisoner by Force Three after being kidnapped from hospital?

45. The designer of the Point Blanc Academy building was shot by its owners, back in the 19th century: true or false?

46. In which book did Alex tightrope-walk away from a burning tower block?

47. What was the car-based nickname of the drug dealer at Alex Rider's school: Ford, Subaru or Skoda?

48. How old was Alex Rider at the start of *Stormbreaker*?

49. What nationality was Ian Rider's housekeeper?

50. How did Alex believe his parents had died?

MEDIUM QUESTIONS

1. Was Sabina's father: a journalist, an MI6 agent, a government scientist or a computer programmer?

2. Who was to be Alex's diving buddy on Flamingo Bay: Tamara, Kolo, Magnus Payne or Paul Drevin?

3. Johnson was a CIA agent sent to Skeleton Key before Alex visited. Did Johnson go undercover as a diving enthusiast, a bird-watcher, a tourist or an archaeologist?

4. What hour is bedtime for the boys at the Point Blanc Academy?

5. What was the name of the 'bank' at which Ian Rider allegedly worked?

6. What lethal virus did each Stormbreaker computer contain?

7. In *Point Blanc*, who lived in Haverstock Hall?

8. Who owned the company that manufactured Stormbreaker computers?

9. What was the name of the acne cream given to Alex by Smithers?

10. What single letter name did Mrs Jones's cat have?

11. Most of the rooms of the second and third floors of Point Blanc were identical to the two floors below except that in the upper floors, there were: televisions, laptop computers or machine guns?

12. What was the name of the man who had appeared on the cover of *Time* magazine and was the ninth or tenth richest man in the world: Edward Pleasure or Michael J. Roscoe?

13. What sort of weapon was General Sarov planning to deploy in Murmansk?

14. What was the only item found in Jerry Harris's fridge in *Scorpia*?

15. Jack accompanied Alex on his first visit to the Royal & General Bank: true or false?

16. How many of Alex's bullets hit Herod Sayle?

17. Mauve and what other colour were the colours of the clothing worn by ball boys and girls at Wimbledon?

18. Was Sarov's estate on Skeleton Key a former tobacco farm, sugar plantation or rum distillery?

19. Who had a banker for a father, put up lots of old sci-fi film posters in his bedroom at Point Blanc and had been thrown out of a school in Düsseldorf?

20. What was the name of the English football club Drevin had bought in *Ark Angel*?

21. What did Alex find in the canopy of the four-poster bed in his room at Sayle's house?

22. Did Herod Sayle intend to give a Stormbreaker to every nursery school, secondary school or university in the country?

23. Was Eric Graves, Charles Pieri or Marc Antonio the name of the photographer Edward Pleasure stayed with shortly before joining his family on holiday in France?

24. Had Alex Rider's soup, dessert or drink been drugged when dining with Mrs Stellenbosch in Paris?

25. The night Alex was locked into his room at Point Blanc, how did he get out?

26. Who used the trolley as a battering ram to attack Damian Cray on Air Force One?

27. Who was the first schoolboy Alex told about his life as a spy?

28. What part of Alex's body was bandaged when Mrs Jones visited him in hospital in Grenoble?

29. What did the briefcase given to Max Grendel by Mrs Rothman contain?

30. What was the name of the new but nasty Chinese triad that Alex crossed paths with near the start of *Skeleton Key*?

31. What was the first weapon Alex managed to get his character to grab when playing Feathered Serpent at the Gameslayer launch?

32. When disguised as a pizza delivery boy, what item was Alex's gun hidden in?

33. Herod Sayle told Alex that the stinging cells of the jellyfish were called: toxiplasts, palmenatoma or nematocysts?

34. At which football stadium did Alex watch a game as a guest of Nikolei Drevin?

35. In the Stormbreaker computer, was the compartment containing the virus above the screen, in the keyboard or in the mouse?

36. At which British airport did Cray and his team take over Air Force One?

37. What weapon did Smithers's inhaler turn into if the cylinder was twisted round twice clockwise?

38. To what American city was Drevin trying to redirect Ark Angel?

39. What meat was the first dinner Alex ate at Sir David Friend's house: pork, ostrich or venison?

40. Which character in *Skeleton Key* ate eggs raw: General Sarov, Turner or Conrad?

41. Who tried to exit Point Blanc in their helicopter when the SAS attacked?

42. Adam Wright was given what item of jewellery by members of Force Three?

43. What three-digit number did Alex have to dial on his mobile phone to fire a drugged dart?

44. How much money did Carlo and Marc ask General Sarov for, in addition to what he had paid them: quarter of a million, half a million or one million dollars?

45. Into which company's complex did Alex Rider use a parachute to BASE jump?

46. Which one of the following was not a games cartridge given to Alex in *Stormbreaker*: Nemesis, Chaos or Bomber Boy?

47. Did Tom Harris believe Alex or not, when he told him that he was a spy?

48. Which woman had arranged for a bomb to be put on Alex's parents' flight: Mrs Rothman, Mrs Jones or Mrs Stellenbosch?

49. In which one of the following places did the Friend family in *Point Blanc* not have a property: Barbados, New York, Tokyo, Rome?

50. Did Alex discover the real James Sprintz in the first, second, third or fourth cell he found at Point Blanc?

QUIZ 2

1. Which character in the Alex Rider books was Miss South Africa five times in a row?

2. Alex killed the snake in the game, Feathered Serpent, using what weapon?

3. Did the jet carrying Alex and General Sarov land in Moscow, Kiev, Murmansk or Bratislava?

4. Can you name either of the two people James Sprintz called Darth Vader and King Kong?

5. What drink did Alex ask for the first time he entered Crawley's office?

6. Was the man who flew jumbo jets in *Eagle Strike* Henryk, Harald, Harvey or Hubert?

7. How old was Alex when he had first learned karate?

8. The killer of Michael Roscoe used the identity of a lift engineer to gain entry into Roscoe Tower. Was the name: Bill Scarlet, Sam Green, Jim Brown or Greg Lime?

9. How many guards did Alex make inoperative by using his special insect-attracting substance from Smithers?

10. Who stole the flash drive from Damian Cray's office desk?

11. Was Sarov's nuclear bomb operated by a key, a codepad or a plastic card?

12. Does Dr Grief say that Joe Canterbury, Hugo Vries or James Sprintz may one day become the President of the United States?

13. Who did Professor Yermalov say were the greatest of all spies: the Russians, the Japanese ninjas, the Gurkhas or the Ancient Romans?

14. What colour was the clothing of the guards at Point Blanc?

15. Whilst Alex was in hospital, who sent him a teddy bear card that talked before self-destructing?

16. Was Alex first told that his uncle died on Euston Road, Old Street, Park Lane or the M25?

17. Ian Rider turned out to be a field agent working for: MI6, CIA, MI5 or the FBI?

18. How many board members of Scorpia were still alive by the time Alex went into training with them?

19. Someone who Blunt and Mrs Jones had told Alex about emerged from the submarine in *Stormbreaker*; who was it?

20. Which member of the Pleasure family was seriously injured by a bomb attack on their holiday home?

21. Which eco-terrorist group had blown up a research centre in New Zealand and a car-making plant in the United States?

22. Is Point Blanc Academy nearest to Grenoble, Toulouse or Zurich?

23. For which secret service does Alex work in the book *Skeleton Key*?

24. At Brookland School, what colour was the blazer that Alex wore?

25. Did Alex have to wait five, ten, twenty or thirty seconds for the Michael Owen figure given to him by Smithers to work?

26. Who pretended to be an Italian called Federico Casali to get through security at Heathrow Airport?

27. What was the maximum speed of Drevin's go-karts: 60, 80 or 100 mph?

28. Who gave Alex two devices for defensive measures not approved by Mr Blunt?

29. The first board meeting of Scorpia took place in an ice cream parlour: true or false?

30. At the end of *Eagle Strike*, is the Pleasure family moving to Tokyo, New York, Rome or San Francisco?

31. What was the name of Alex's tutor in the book *Scorpia*?

32. What name is given to the amazingly powerful new processor inside the Stormbreaker?

33. Did the crane Alex operated in *Point Blanc* have a maximum lifting capacity of: 1450kg, 2200kg, 2750kg or 3900kg?

34. Whose office was next to Ian Rider's at the Royal & General Bank?

35. Whose handbag did the bag snatchers take in Venice at the start of *Scorpia*?

36. Alex's cover on visiting Skeleton Key had him born in Chicago, California, Florida or New York?

37. Was Owen Bryant an Australian, English or American tennis player?

38. In *Point Blanc*, who had telephoned Blunt the day before he was killed?

39. What was the first name of the person who lent Alex the equipment to BASE jump in *Scorpia*?

40. In *Point Blanc*, how many hundred steps were on the ladder up to the crane driver's cab?

41. What government appointment in South Africa did Dr Grief get even though he was only in his twenties?

42. Did the kidnappers in *Ark Angel* intend to send back an ear, a finger, a toe or some hair of Alex's?

43. Cray's flash drive is the key to America's nuclear missiles. Does Cray say he will have 500, 1000, 2000 or 2500 nuclear missiles under his control?

44. After travelling through the tin mine tunnels, was the first room Alex spied: a guardroom, a laboratory, the assembly line or a prison?

45. At which address did Cobra meetings take place: the White House, the Royal & General Bank, Number 10 Downing Street or New Scotland Yard?

46. At what museum was the Stormbreaker computer to be launched?

47. Out of which part of his uncle's car did Alex crawl to escape being crushed?

48. What was the first name of Sir David Friend's snooty daughter?

49. Were there two, three or six buttons on each of the crane's joysticks in *Point Blanc*?

50. Was Mr Wiseman Alex's maths, history, languages or PE teacher?

1. Was the name of the old Brookland School caretaker, Mr Brown, Mr Lee, Mr Jackson or Mr Phipps?

2. What item given to Alex could be used to see in the dark?

3. What position did John Crawley say he held at the Royal & General Bank?

4. What did Cray tell Alex was the single biggest evil in the world today: communism, America, drugs or classical music?

5. What colour was the torpedo-shaped bomb on board Ark Angel?

6. In *Eagle Strike*, who grabbed Alex as he was pointing the gun at Yassen Gregorovich?

7. In which book does Alex foil an attempt to detonate a bomb in the Kola Peninsula?

8. Was a Colibri EC120B: a machine gun, a flamethrower or a helicopter?

9. In *Scorpia*, who made a tiger fall asleep with the press of a remote control button?

10. Did Sabina visit her father in St Anne's, Stoke Mandeville or Whitchurch hospital?

11. *Cayo Esqueleto* is the Spanish name for what island where Alex had several adventures?

12. What did Dr Karl Steiner say the injection that he gave Alex was?

13. What was the name of the giant wave seen only occasionally off the coast of Cornwall?

14. Who turned out to have paid for and ordered the deaths of Michael Roscoe and General Ivanov: Alan Blunt, Skoda, Dr Grief or Yassen Gregorovich?

15. In *Scorpia*, Alex rejoined Tom on board a train bound for which Italian city?

16. Can you name two of the five boys who made up the shooting party that Alex and Fiona joined?

17. What was the first gadget Smithers showed Alex: the Game Boy, the zit cream or the yo-yo?

18. Scorpia's demands letter insists that which politician must resign: the British Prime Minister, the US President or the head of the United Nations?

19. The Crimean Star was a luxury boat owned by Dr Grief, Mr Grin, Damian Cray or Nikolei Drevin?

20. Edmund Hill-Smith was captain of which sports team in the book, *Scorpia*?

21. What nationality was Michael J. Roscoe's secretary?

22. Alex first used the circular saw function of his CD player on a rod fitted to what part of his room in the Point Blanc Academy?

23. Who offered Alex Rider the chance to work for Scorpia?

24. What was Alex's cover name when attending the Point Blanc Academy?

25. How many clones did Dr Grief make of himself?

26. Were the Stormbreaker computers being made in Port Tallon, Port Talbot or Port Meirion?

27. With which government did Drevin build the Ark Angel space hotel?

28. Alex's cover when going to Skeleton Key included having a pet dog at home. Was it called Lucky, Fido, Rufus or Barker?

29. In *Point Blanc*, how many trains an hour did Fiona say ran down the local railway line?

30. What meal did Alex, Turner and Troy have shortly before Turner had to meet the Salesman?

31. Adam Wright had joined Stratford East from which famous football club?

32. After Alex and Sabina had a row outside the Royal & General Bank, who appeared alongside Alex on the pavement?

33. Did Alex join C Force, K Unit or Group X when undergoing training in *Stormbreaker*?

34. General Sarov's son was killed in which Middle Eastern country?

35. What was the title of the famous book given to Alex by Smithers?

36. Who was the first person of his own age Alex Rider knocked out using karate?

37. Fiona took a short-cut home while horse-riding. Was it through a river, a railway tunnel or over a steep hill?

38. Was the name of Damian Cray's white poodle Barker, Bubbles or Curly?

39. Did Alex use a fishing net, a harpoon or a flare gun to help knock Franco unconscious?

40. In what vehicle did the first member of a Chinese triad try to kill Alex while he was underneath the courts at Wimbledon?

41. What weapons were built into the snowmobiles used by Dr Grief's men?

42. What colour uniform did the military force attacking General Sarov's force wear?

43. What was the first item Smithers gave and described to Alex in the book *Point Blanc*?

44. At a bullfight, a *novillero* was: a junior matador, a spear or the fence surrounding the bullring?

45. On what Mediterranean island did MI6 appear to set a trap for Alex's father, according to Mrs Rothman?

46. Who did Alex meet on more than one occasion that turned out to be the man codenamed Cossack at the start of *Eagle Strike*?

47. For which secret service was Tamara Knight working?

48. Where had Alex planned to lower the barge containing Skoda: on Putney Bridge, in the police station car park or on the helicopter landing pad of MI6?

49. Which member of MI6 was on the committee of the All-England Tennis Club, which organizes Wimbledon?

50. To which country had MI6 sent the real Felix Lester on holiday?

QUIZ 4

1. Did Nile say he was twelve, sixteen, eighteen or twenty-two when he killed his first man?

2. How many bullets did the gun given to Alex by Scorpia to kill Mrs Jones contain?

3. Who was hit by the second bullet fired by Cray on board Air Force One?

4. What device used in the Winter Olympics was found at Point Blanc, but was out of bounds?

5. What type of bird flocked to eat the bird seed that covered the bag snatchers in Venice?

6. What was unusual about the photographer Marc Antonio's face?

7. Which device given to Alex by Smithers had a panic button that would send a signal to a satellite?

8. At his press conference, did Nikolei Drevin say that Ark Angel was: £100 million, £200 million, £300 million or £400 million over budget?

9. Who crashed into barbed wire, severely gashing their head, after being thrown from a train?

10. When trapped in the Mary Belle, did Alex use a rifle, an anchor, a sword or a large spanner as a crowbar?

11. Alex stood in front of which Russian who took his own life at the end of *Skeleton Key*?

12. Who was to place the nuclear bomb on the submarine in Murmansk?

13. Which famous real-life singer did Mrs Jones say Damian Cray had sung with as a boy at the Royal Academy of Music?

14. What was the name of the company manufacturing Stormbreakers?

15. Damian Cray's garden contained models of famous buildings built to 1/100th scale. Can you name any one of the buildings?

16. What computer game console did Turner give Alex before they flew to Skeleton Key?

17. Who offered to make the BASE jump in *Scorpia* instead of Alex?

18. In *Skeleton Key*, which Russian city is home to the northern fleet of Russian submarines?

19. What was the name of the board member of Scorpia who announced he was retiring?

20. What was the name of Alex's maths teacher?

21. One of the quad bikers was injured in the electrocuted fence. How did the other perish?

22. What is the only method of transport possible to and from Point Blanc?

23. Which classical composer's CD converted Alex's CD player into a saw?

24. Who confronted Alex in the dining room when Alex was part of the SAS attack on Point Blanc?

25. In which city was Alex when he was shot by a sniper at the end of one of the books?

26. What part of Sabina's body did Cray threaten to have cut off unless Alex returned the flash drive?

27. Who told Nikolei Drevin that Alex was a spy?

28. What part of the Prime Minister did Alex Rider hit with a bullet?

29. Which member of Force Three did Alex hit with an oxygen cylinder: Combat Jacket, Steel Watch or Spectacles?

30. What weapon did Wolf use to neutralize the first guard at Point Blanc?

31. Whose conversation did Alex first listen to using his eavesdropping device from Smithers, when on Flamingo Bay?

32. Who was the director of the Point Blanc Academy?

33. Before surfing with Sabina in *Skeleton Key* Alex had been surfing before, at which two of the following places: Florida, Cornwall, Norfolk, Barbados or California?

34. Who was Edward Pleasure writing an article about in the book *Eagle Strike*?

35. Who did Alex ask to press the self-destruct button to stop the nuclear missiles launched by Cray?

36. Was Turner pretending to buy weapons, uranium, drugs or counterfeit money from the Salesman?

37. Did Michael Roscoe die by: falling down a lift shaft, being shot in the back, being poisoned or being stabbed?

38. What was the name of the French tennis player Alex watched cause two upsets by beating more favoured players at Wimbledon?

39. How many metres of special nylon did Alex's yo-yo hold: ten, thirty, sixty or one hundred metres?

40. In *Stormbreaker*, Alex was ordered not to parachute whilst training in Wales because of a signal from London: true or false?

41. Which member of K Unit spoke with a Scottish accent?

42. In *Ark Angel*, knockout gas could be released from what item when it was pressed?

43. Which one of the following did General Sarov's house not have: tennis court, giant chessboard, swimming pool or sauna?

44. Was the name of General Sarov's son: Dimitry, Boris or Vladimir?

45. What was the name of the small, plump man in Scorpia with a black beard, grey hair and gold-rimmed glasses?

46. In *Eagle Strike* was Tlaloc, Xipe Totec or Xolotl an Aztec god with his eyeballs hanging out?

47. Dieter Sprintz was known as the One Hundred Million Dollar Man. How long had it taken him to make that sum of money?

48. Which one of the following did Alex not have as part of his disguise as a pizza delivery boy: a gold tooth, a beard, a pair of thick glasses, motorcycle leathers?

49. A visit to which funfair, Blackpool, Swanage or Putney, inspired Alex to use the crane in *Point Blanc*?

50. The day Alex returned home in *Ark Angel*, who phoned to invite him to tea?

QUIZ 5

1. Did Dr Grief say he was eleven, fourteen, seventeen or twenty-three the first time he attended a human dissection?

2. In *Stormbreaker*, how many hairs did Alex put across the zip of his sports bag so he could check that no one had opened it?

3. Was caviar, shark steak or prawn cocktail the first food served at General Sarov's dinner for the Russian President?

4. Who did Nikolei Drevin shoot by mistake when he had intended to kill Alex?

5. What was the first name of Fraülein Vole in *Stormbreaker*?

6. Who gave the radio command for the security men protecting the Prime Minister in the Science Museum not to shoot Alex?

7. Did Paul Drevin's home in Oxfordshire have one, two or no swimming pools?

8. In *Stormbreaker*, who did the authorities say was hit by a lorry when not wearing a seat-belt?

9. In what ocean did the space capsule carrying Alex land?

10. What was the name of the NSA staff member who sold secrets to Damian Cray?

11. Did Alex have to count to five, ten, thirty or sixty before his explosive earring from Smithers worked?

12. In *Point Blanc*, how many seats did the Robinson R44 helicopter have?

13. Who sneaked a note into Alex's clothing after he had been caught by MI6 for his attempt to kill Mrs Jones?

14. How many docking ports did Ark Angel have?

15. What was the name of the project, beginning with the letter G, run by Dr Hugo Grief?

16. How many minutes did Fiona say it took to ride through the train tunnel near Haverstock Hall?

17. Was Herod Sayle born in Dubai, Kabul, Cairo or Beirut?

18. What was the name of the civil servant whose son John Rider had saved many years ago: Alan Blunt, Mrs Jones, Sir Graham Adair or Mark Kellner?

19. Who took Alex on his first ever kite surfing session?

20. The Royal Route was an underground tunnel which connected the Millennium Building at Wimbledon to: Centre Court, Number One Court or Number Two Court?

21. Was Felix Lester's father a police inspector, a jewellery designer or an architect?

22. Who did Alex Rider hit with his fifth and sixth bullets in the Science Museum in *Stormbreaker*?

23. What sort of aircraft was Air Force One?

24. Sir Arthur Lunt had made his fortune building what sort of structure: bridges, hotels, multi-storey car parks or banks?

25. Was Alex refused entry at Heathrow, JFK or Rome Airport due to his passport having expired?

26. Centurion International Advertizing was the sign on a building belonging to which secret service?

27. Alex had gone diving with his uncle, Ian Rider, off which Caribbean island: Tobago, Barbados, Jamaica or Guadeloupe?

28. What military medal did Alex's father win for bravery in the Falkland Islands conflict?

29. What was the family name that Troy, Turner and Alex adopted when visiting Skeleton Key?

30. What did the Speed Wars cartridge turn Alex's portable games device into?

31. In *Skeleton Key*, what creatures killed and ate the men inside the Cessna plane trapped in the swamp?

32. In *Stormbreaker*, who turned out to be piloting the cargo plane Alex managed to stow away in?

33. How many years had Mr Grin worked for Herod Sayle?

34. What was the name of the house in Venice where Mrs Rothman lived?

35. Which character in *Skeleton Key* was number four on the CIA's most wanted list?

36. Who did Alan Blunt say would have to leave England if Alex didn't work for MI6?

37. Who tried to escape from Flamingo Bay in a Cessna light aircraft?

38. What part of Tamara Knight's clothing contained diamond-edged tungsten wire able to cut through steel?

39. Puerto Madre was the second biggest town on Grief Island, Skeleton Key, Point Blanc or Haiti?

40. Whose receipt from a bookshop near to the CIA headquarters provoked suspicion from the airport security staff at Skeleton Key?

41. In which country was Point Blanc Academy?

42. What shape was the red tattoo on the arm of the guard at Wimbledon?

43. Who was the first person Alex recognized in the Consanto Enterprises complex: Mrs Rothman, Nile, Alan Blunt or Dr Liebermann?

44. In *Point Blanc*, which former KGB man was killed in a boating accident on the Black Sea: Drevin, Sarov or Ivanov?

45. Can you name one of the three games Alex spies in the games room at Point Blanc?

46. What structure did Alex and Fiona leap off to avoid being crushed by the train?

47. The night that Alex entered and escaped Cray's software plant, Yassen Gregorovich had been learning which foreign language?

48. Was Alex in Puerto Madre, Santiago Airport or in the water around Skeleton Key when he saw Troy and Turner for the last time?

49. Which pop star had started the Chart Attack charity?

50. Who did Scorpia ask Alex to kill first: Alan Blunt, the Deputy Prime Minister, Jack Starbright or Mrs Jones?

QUIZ 6

1. Whose office number at the Royal & General Bank was 1504?

2. Who decides to wait twenty-four hours after Alex has pressed the panic button in *Point Blanc*?

3. What was the name of the sunken transport ship that Alex was to dive and see in the book *Ark Angel*?

4. How quickly did Wolf manage to complete the assault course with K Unit: twelve, fourteen, sixteen or eighteen minutes?

5. Which one of the following items was not in the hold of the sunken Mary Belle ship: a pile of rifles, a tank, a jeep, a row of boots?

6. How many metal studs did Skoda have in his ear?

7. Were Turner and Troy delighted, unhappy or indifferent about working with Alex?

8. Which contract killer did Alex spot on a yacht when he was holidaying in France with the Pleasure family?

9. In which month did Alex first meet Mrs Jones?

10. Who had beaten Stratford East 3-0 in the game before the one that Alex attended?

11. Which member of Force Three did Alex attack with a defibrillator: Combat Jacket, Silver Tooth or Spectacles?

12. The crane in *Point Blanc* checked for body heat before switching on: true or false?

13. In *Ark Angel*, was the burning building that Alex was trapped in part of a new complex called: Dockside, Riverview or Hornchurch Towers?

14. In the communications centre of Air Force One, there were two buttons used for firing the nuclear missiles. One was to launch the missiles, what words were printed on the other?

15. What sort of music had Ian Rider liked?

16. Scorpia's letter includes the demand that one billion dollars must be paid, into which bank?

17. Of the seven boys at the Point Blanc Academy, how many were American?

18. Who hired a tutor for Alex as he started slipping behind at school?

19. What item did Alex send hurtling down the ski slope to crash into Dr Grief's helicopter?

20. What was the name of the principal who headed Scorpia's Training and Assessment Center?

21. How many days after their marriage had Mrs Rothman's husband died: two, fourteen, twenty-eight or forty?

22. In the Feathered Serpent game, which zone came first: the mirror maze, the pit with the flying creature or the pool of fire?

23. Did air, water or fire cause Adam Wright's new piece of jewellery to react violently and explode, killing him?

24. Was the name of Alex's personal guard at Sarov's house: Juan, Michel, Carlos or Pedro?

25. At what age would the money held in trust for Alex be available to him?

26. What did Alex do immediately after pressing the panic button on his CD player in *Point Blanc*?

27. Who prepared a number of files on the Friend family background for Alex to read and learn?

28. Was Damian Cray to pay Charlie Roper a total of $2.5 million, $4.5 million, $6 million or $9 million?

29. Which spy gadget given to him in *Stormbreaker* did Alex use to gain entry into the crane driver's cab in *Point Blanc*?

30. The Dragon Head is the leader of what criminal group?

31. Did Herod Sayle have one, three, four or seven sisters?

32. What was the name, beginning with the letter G, of the local man who piloted the boat which carried Turner, Troy and Alex towards Casa de Oro?

33. In whose Royal & General Bank office was Alex when he was shot by a drugged dart?

34. In *Scorpia*, the homing device Smithers gave Alex was disguised as: a pair of sunglasses, a baseball cap, a signet ring or a teeth brace?

35. How many nuclear missiles did Cray launch in *Eagle Strike*?

36. What business, situated on Lambeth Walk, did Alex visit shortly after his uncle's funeral?

37. What was the name of Nikolei Drevin's personal assistant?

38. In *Scorpia*, the England reserve football team were flying back after playing games in which African country?

39. In *Eagle Strike*, did Alex learn about Sabina's disappearance from: a newspaper at the airport, a phone message at home or Mrs Jones at MI6?

40. How many O-levels did Herod Sayle get?

41. Which Point Blanc staff member received the news at the Grenoble hospital that Alex Rider was dead?

42. Which friend of Alex's had once spent a year studying art in Paris?

43. Who did Alex see killing Dr Baxter?

44. Whose metal-filled body attracted the magnets on the crane in the Russian shipyard, saving Alex from certain death?

45. What was the only room in the house where Alex lived that was usually locked?

46. What did Alex use to breathe through when hiding in the lake?

47. What metal did Force Three tell Adam Wright that their jewellery gift to him was made of: caesium, magnesium, platinum or plutonium?

48. What was the name of the new computer games system created by Cray Software Technology?

49. How many black limousines carried the Russian President's group to General Sarov's house?

50. Which member of MI6 came to visit Alex in hospital after he escaped from the burning building?

QUIZ 7

1. What single letter did Ian Rider send back as a code in his last ever message?

2. What was Alex's room number at the Paris hotel in *Point Blanc*?

3. Which American city did Alex fly into to meet Troy and Turner?

4. Who arranged for Professor Milburn to be killed because he ran an institute in which animals were used for cosmetics testing?

5. How many boats chased Alex as he tried to escape from Flamingo Bay?

6. Was the chief constable of the Metropolitan Police giving a speech about drugs near the start of *Point Blanc*, *Eagle Strike* or *Stormbreaker*?

7. On which two floors of the Point Blanc building was Alex told he was allowed?

8. The odds on Jacques Lefevre winning Wimbledon were 80-1, 125-1, 200-1 or 300-1?

9. Who visited Alex in hospital twice a day in the book *Ark Angel*?

10. In which month is the Stormbreaker to be launched?

11. What game did Alan Blunt and Sir Graham Adair play together occasionally: chess, poker, bridge or billiards?

12. What was Agent Turner's first name?

13. Whose father was a failed hairdresser in *Stormbreaker*?

14. Was the cargo plane in *Stormbreaker* over Swindon, Reading or Windsor when Alex had put on the parachute?

15. According to Mrs Jones, how many years had Point Blanc Academy been in existence?

16. How long would it take for the nuclear missiles launched by Cray to reach their target: 60 minutes, 90 minutes, 120 minutes or 180 minutes?

17. In *Scorpia*, who used a samurai knife to kill someone by aiming through the neck into the brain?

18. What creature in *Scorpia* could eat one hundred pounds of meat in one go?

19. What sort of spider threatened to kill the young assassin at the very start of *Eagle Strike*: a black widow, a tarantula or a trapdoor spider?

20. What was the name on the sign of the building under construction close to Putney Bridge where Alex found Skoda's drugs-making laboratory?

21. Which of the boys at Point Blanc was a vegetarian: James Sprintz, Hugo Vries or Joe Canterbury?

22. How long was the hike Alex and K Unit had to go on: fifteen, twenty, thirty-two or forty kilometres?

23. Was the Fer de Lance: an award for valour, a boat or a castle in France?

24. On which floor did Alex find a number of children locked up at Point Blanc?

25. What material would the acne cream given to Alex cut through in seconds?

26. *Sai-lo* means big brother, little brother or leader?

27. In which English county would you find the village of Port Tallon?

28. Sloterdijk was the location of one of Cray's many businesses in *Eagle Strike*; in what country was Sloterdijk?

29. Was Alex's father in the Paras, the SAS, the SBS or the regular army infantry?

30. How many musicians played classical music at the dinner hosted by General Sarov for the President of Russia?

31. Of the boys at Point Blanc, was Nicolas Marc, Tom McCorin or Cassian James Canadian?

32. Who was hit by the first shot fired by Cray on board Air Force One?

33. What objects did Alex tie to Drevin's light aircraft to hinder its getaway?

34. Which member of Scorpia gave Alex a thorough strip search to check that he was carrying no bugs?

35. What was the first London landmark Alex recognized when he was in the cargo plane from Cornwall?

36. Did Alex hurt his ankle, wrist or knee when being chased by the quad bikers in *Stormbreaker*?

37. Which boy did Alex hear being dragged protesting, the night he escaped from his bedroom: Paul Roscoe, Hugo Vries or James Sprintz?

38. How many of the trainees at Scorpia's training centre were women: none, two, four or eight?

39. What was the first name of the former close friend of Alex's who had changed due to becoming addicted to drugs?

40. How many visitors came to Alex's house the day he learned his uncle had died?

41. Was Marc Antonio's photographic studio on rue Anglais, rue Deschamps or rue Britannia?

42. How much did Mrs Rothman tell the other members of Scorpia had been paid into their Swiss bank account: five, ten, twenty or fifty million pounds?

43. What colour was the bedroom Alex was using while he stayed at Sayle's house?

44. At Scorpia's training centre did the Thai lady called Jet teach: explosives, martial arts or botany?

45. What did Alex use to break the aquarium holding the giant jellyfish?

46. Did a woman, a bearded man or a small boy ask Damian Cray why his computer games contained violence at the launch of Gameslayer?

47. Did Drevin make a donation of one, two, three or five million pounds to the hospital that Alex and Paul had stayed in?

48. Who did Nile kill in front of Alex at the Consanto Enterprises complex?

49. What device on Alex's new bike produced a smokescreen?

50. Which one of the following celebrities did Alex not see in a photograph posing with Nikolei Drevin: Tom Cruise, Nelson Mandela, Julia Roberts or Elton John?

1. Professor Yermalov was an unfriendly instructor in which Alex Rider book?

2. What is the funny name of the bubblegum that Smithers gives Alex?

3. After the bullfight did Alex require three stitches on his forehead, his arm, his stomach or his bottom?

4. What football team were Nikolei Drevin's team playing when Alex attended the game?

5. What colour clothing was Omni wearing in the Gameslayer games?

6. Can you name either of the adults who were on the school trip to Venice?

7. In *Point Blanc* what item did Alex turn into a snowboard?

8. Which ultra-rich but evil man had had an entire convent building shipped from Italy to the south of England?

9. Did Alex have a cut on his left arm, right leg, forehead or chest which attracted the shark to attack in *Skeleton Key*?

10. How did Alex gain entry to the second and third floor of Point Blanc for the first time?

11. Did Conrad, the President of Russia or Agent Turner say that Alex reminded him of General Sarov's son?

12. In *Skeleton Key*, who lived in Casa de Oro?

13. How many of the SAS personnel used in the attack on Point Blanc were killed?

14. Which cartridge turned Alex's games machines into a fax and photocopier?

15. Terahertz beams were used by which criminal organization to release poisons into peoples' bodies?

16. What was the name of the airport on Skeleton Key that Alex and the others flew into?

17. What sort of vehicle was parked outside Alex's house as he returned from his uncle's funeral?

18. The second time Alex used a karate move in *Stormbreaker*, he managed to disarm: a guard, Nadia Vole, Herod Sayle or Yassen Gregorovich?

19. Which member of Alex's family had been a radiology nurse and had the first name, Helen?

20. Approximately how old was Joe Byrne: forty, fifty, sixty or seventy?

21. In *Ark Angel*, what items did Alex use on the end of his tightrope pole to balance it?

22. Behind what object in his bedroom in Sayle's house did Alex discover a bug?

23. Alex had bruises around his neck from which character in *Skeleton Key* trying to strangle him?

24. Which one of the following was not a member of K Unit: Fox, Wolf or Lizard?

25. Was Conrad born in Albania, Turkey, Germany or Cuba?

26. When Alex started training as a spy did he hike in the Scottish Highlands, the Brecon Beacons or the Lake District?

27. Who visited Alex at the end of *Skeleton Key* to invite him to France?

28. Which member of the Friend family knew nothing about Alex's work as a spy?

29. What was the name of the schoolboy who won the prize to be the first to use a Stormbreaker computer?

30. Did Alex's father turn out to be the brother of Damian Cray, a contract killer, still alive and working for the KGB or an agent of MI6?

31. Alex performed *Ushiro-geri* on a man at the breaker's yard. Was it a kung fu, kickboxing or karate move?

32. In *Eagle Strike*, did Alex have a holiday with Sabina and her family in France, Spain or Italy?

33. After using the Stormbreaker, Alex returned to Herod Sayle's house to find him playing which game?

34. What subject did the librarian say that Alex's uncle had researched in Port Tallon: viruses, robotics, industrial sabotage or Lebanese history?

35. What substance did Alex threaten to destroy Cray's flash drive with if Sabina wasn't released?

36. What was the make of the Japanese snowmobiles used by Dr Grief's men in *Point Blanc*?

37. What was the first name of Nikolei Drevin's only son?

38. Alex's first slip-up with Herod Sayle was to: use his own name, reveal he knew what Sayle's father did or to reveal too much about the Stormbreaker?

39. How did Alex plan to leave Sarov's house when Sarov and the others went to Santiago?

40. At the end of their game of snooker, did Herod Sayle owe Alex £270, £700, £1200 or £4100?

41. Who set off the explosives that destroyed the Consanto Enterprises complex?

42. On what sort of vehicle were Skoda and his colleague preparing drugs?

43. How many million euros was Dr Liebermann being paid by Scorpia: one, five, ten or fifteen?

44. Which member of the shooting party did Alex knock to the ground with the shotgun?

45. What part of his body bled slightly after Alex successfully completed the BASE jump?

46. In *Point Blanc* which item given to Alex by Smithers fired a stun dart?

47. What was the name of the assassin who Blunt thought killed Ian Rider?

48. Which knight pretended to be Alex's father in *Point Blanc*?

49. CL 475/19 was a vital clue discovered by Alex, left by which character?

50. In *Skeleton Key*, did the Cubans, CIA, MI6 or the Russians find their President locked up in General Sarov's house?

QUIZ 9

1. Did Jerry receive a cheque worth: one, three, five or seven thousand euros for his destroyed BASE jumping equipment?

2. In *Stormbreaker*, how many beds were usually found in each hut at the spy training camp Alex attended?

36. What was the make of the Japanese snowmobiles used by Dr Grief's men in *Point Blanc*?

37. What was the first name of Nikolei Drevin's only son?

38. Alex's first slip-up with Herod Sayle was to: use his own name, reveal he knew what Sayle's father did or to reveal too much about the Stormbreaker?

39. How did Alex plan to leave Sarov's house when Sarov and the others went to Santiago?

40. At the end of their game of snooker, did Herod Sayle owe Alex £270, £700, £1200 or £4100?

41. Who set off the explosives that destroyed the Consanto Enterprises complex?

42. On what sort of vehicle were Skoda and his colleague preparing drugs?

43. How many million euros was Dr Liebermann being paid by Scorpia: one, five, ten or fifteen?

44. Which member of the shooting party did Alex knock to the ground with the shotgun?

45. What part of his body bled slightly after Alex successfully completed the BASE jump?

46. In *Point Blanc* which item given to Alex by Smithers fired a stun dart?

47. What was the name of the assassin who Blunt thought killed Ian Rider?

48. Which knight pretended to be Alex's father in *Point Blanc*?

49. CL 475/19 was a vital clue discovered by Alex, left by which character?

50. In *Skeleton Key*, did the Cubans, CIA, MI6 or the Russians find their President locked up in General Sarov's house?

QUIZ 9

1. Did Jerry receive a cheque worth: one, three, five or seven thousand euros for his destroyed BASE jumping equipment?

2. In *Stormbreaker*, how many beds were usually found in each hut at the spy training camp Alex attended?

3. Who did Alex meet in the headmaster's office at the end of *Point Blanc*?

4. Did the green, blue or grey button on Alex's bike release a trail of slippery slime?

5. Who collected Alex and Turner in a speedboat when they were in the water not far from Miami?

6. Which member of the Friend family did Alex encounter first?

7. Which member of MI6 met Alex after he played a game of football in *Skeleton Key*?

8. The first time Alex and Franco fought in *Eagle Strike*, what weapon did Franco have?

9. What school team was Tom Harris the captain of?

10. Joe Byrne was deputy director for operations in which secret service?

11. Cray's plan to get the airport evacuated included pretending that an aircraft was carrying: nuclear weapons, nerve gas or crates of dynamite?

12. Where did Alex order Mr Grin to fly the hijacked plane?

13. Alex and Jack stayed in the Saskia Hotel in Amsterdam in which book?

14. For how many million pounds had Drevin bought Stratford East football club?

15. What was the name of the man who carried out the examination of Alex when he was drugged in a Paris hotel?

16. Stratford East's football strip was black and what other colour?

17. How many thousand pounds a term did it cost to send a boy to Point Blanc Academy?

18. What colour button did Alex press on his bike to send out two heat-seeking missiles?

19. In *Skeleton Key*, what was the name of the man who had half his head bald, a permanently bloodshot eye and walked in a strange way?

20. Which member of the Force Three group was waiting for Alex at the bottom of the burning tower block?

21. In *Point Blanc*, how many seconds would it take for the stun dart to knock out an adult, according to Smithers?

22. At the end of *Stormbreaker*, Mrs Jones handed Alex Rider an envelope. Did it contain a cheque, a certificate of commendation or a sick note from a doctor?

23. Who had first taken Alex to the circus?

24. How many weapons were found in the first zone of the Feathered Serpent game?

25. Was General Sarov heading to Moscow, Skeleton Key, London or New York after planting the nuclear bomb?

26. Wally Walfor was: in charge of ball boys and girls at Wimbledon, the assistant director of MI6, the Home Secretary or a cover name given to Alex?

27. Was Dr Three American, Chinese, German or South African?

28. What telltale marks did Alex discover on his uncle's car to prove that his death had not been an accident?

29. In *Skeleton Key*, what item in Alex's luggage turned out to be a Geiger counter?

30. What was a Cannondale Bad Boy?

31. After Alex was first caught by Damian Cray, did Cray give him a glass of vodka, chocolate milk, cranberry juice or lemonade?

32. In *Ark Angel*, did Alex put the bomb in the galley, in the toilet or in the command centre?

33. What two colours were the Sayle Enterprises signs and logos?

34. What was Herod Sayle posing as in order to trap Alex near the end of *Stormbreaker*?

35. Did Alex count approximately ten, twenty, thirty or forty armed guards at Point Blanc?

36. Just before the barge was lifted into the air, Skoda was opening a bottle of what sort of alcohol?

37. Who was killed by being trapped in a glass cubicle filled with millions of coins?

38. Who fired two anaesthetic darts to neutralize two of Dr Grief's guards in the basement of Point Blanc?

39. In which London park did Alex land after clinging on to the hot air balloon in the book *Scorpia*?

40. What was the name of the security specialist killed at the start of *Ark Angel*: Max Webber, Michael Roscoe or Paul Fox?

41. Was arsenic, cyanide or thallium the poison that killed the footballers in the book, *Scorpia*?

42. In what part of her body did Tamara take a bullet whilst on Flamingo Bay: her leg, her shoulder, her stomach or her arm?

43. Which block at Sayle Enterprises housed the main assembly line for the Stormbreaker computer: Block A, B or D?

44. On which birthday had Alex been given the bike he rode in *Stormbreaker*?

45. Who did Yassen Gregorovich kill at the very end of *Stormbreaker*?

46. Alex had learned lots of Spanish when he spent most of a year in Madrid, Malaga, Barcelona or Valencia?

47. In *Stormbreaker*, what was Alex handcuffed to all night at Sayle's house?

48. How many sixteen-year-old bullies had set upon Alex when he first arrived at Brookland School?

49. According to Mr Grin, what was the record for someone surviving in the tank with the giant jellyfish: two hours, five and a half hours or seven hours?

50. In how many of the six Alex Rider novels did Alex meet CIA operative, Joe Byrne?

QUIZ 10

1. Magnus Payne was the head of security on which island?

2. After his attempt at killing Mrs Jones failed, who did Alex have breakfast with?

3. What was the name of the rich businessman killed at the beginning of *Point Blanc*?

4. How many people guarded the last zone of the real-life version of Feathered Serpent?

5. The falling platform from the balloon crushed and killed which character in *Scorpia*?

6. In which war had the Mary Belle ship been sunk: World War I, World War II, the Vietnam War or the Falklands War?

7. The Han Class 404 SSN Alex spotted in *Stormbreaker* was what type of device: a submarine, a machine gun or a rocket launcher?

8. Were there originally six, nine, twelve or fourteen members of the executive board of Scorpia?

9. Were K Unit given two, four or six hours less to complete the survival hike than Alex?

10. How did Dr Grief plan to kill Alex Rider: by dissecting him alive, by shooting him or by casting him out on the cold mountain with no clothes?

11. Were the boys at the Point Blanc Academy allowed to write letters to, email or telephone their parents?

12. Who did Alex Rider shoot with the stun dart from his book in *Point Blanc*?

13. Did Baxter ask Dr Grief for a bonus of: 10,000, 100,000, 200,000 or 500,000 US dollars?

14. Before *Point Blanc* had Alex been snowboarding once, twice, three times or never?

15. Which button had to be pressed three times to activate the panic signal to the satellite in *Point Blanc*?

16. Was the snake, the flying razor boomerang or flying spears the first dangerous feature Alex encountered when playing the real-life version of Feathered Serpent?

17. Was the head of the Metropolitan Police, the Deputy Prime Minister or the head of the United Nations holding a conference at the Putney Riverside Conference Centre in *Point Blanc*?

18. Was the Stormbreaker's round processor one millimetre, half a centimetre or one centimetre in diameter?

19. How many floors high was the Point Blanc building?

20. What device did Alex use to leap on to the Mayfair Lady at Bayside Marketplace?

21. At a bullfight, a *banderilla* was: a junior matador, a spear or the fence surrounding the bullring?

22. How many game cartridges did Alex receive from Smithers?

23. What was the name of the boy Alex met at Point Blanc who was wearing an old Star Wars T-shirt and had bruises on his face from fighting?

24. What was the Russian-based codename of the nineteen-year-old man who was on his first 'kill' at the start of *Eagle Strike*?

25. How often did Alex take karate lessons: once a week, once a fortnight or once a month?

26. What metal item did Mrs Stellenbosch bend in two to show her strength?

27. Kaspar was the commanding officer of which eco-warrior terrorist group?

28. What was the name of the first game available for the Gameslayer computer system?

29. What colour hair did Jack Starbright have?

30. Was a C-130 Hercules, a Beechcraft Baron, a Lockheed Galaxy or a Westland Sea King the vehicle which took Alex Rider's coffin back from France to England in *Point Blanc*?

31. What electrical item did Jack find in the sitting room after she and Alex had returned with Cray's flash drive from Europe?

32. Who refused to kill Sabina and Alex on board Air Force One?

33. Did Jerry Harris live in the Spanish quarter of Rome, Turin, Amalfi or Naples?

34. In which country is Skeleton Key situated?

35. Can you name any one of the three crimes that were on Alex's fake criminal record in *Point Blanc*?

36. The French police first stated that the explosion at the Pleasures' holiday home was caused by: a terrorist bomb, a gas leak or a faulty boiler?

37. What sort of aircraft did Alex fly in when he watched K Unit undergo parachute training: a 707, a C-130 a SR71 or a B-100?

38. In *Ark Angel*, who convincingly beat Alex in two sets of tennis?

39. Where were the buttons that launched secret features hidden on the bike given to Alex by Smithers?

40. What part of Alex's body was the first to be touched by the giant jellyfish, but was fortunately protected?

41. How many times was Wolf hit by bullets from Mrs Stellenbosch's gun?

42. In what vehicle did Mrs Stellenbosch arrive to take Alex to Point Blanc?

43. Who is expected to get British Citizenship as a result of a seemingly generous gift in *Stormbreaker*?

44. Who planned to feed Alex into a sugar cane crusher before he was stopped by General Sarov?

45. At the Point Blanc Academy students were forbidden to bring which two of the following: rock music, a CD player, their own books or laptop computers?

46. When Alex sat down for dinner with the Russian president, was the table set for three, seven or thirteen people?

47. Which member of K Unit called Alex 'Double O Nothing'?

48. Which character in *Scorpia* suffers from vitiligo and has white and black skin?

49. What was the first weapon Alex picked up in the real-life version of Feathered Serpent?

50. Which member of MI6 wondered whether they should tell Alex all they knew about Yassen Gregorovich?

QUIZ 11

1. Who told Alex in Saint-Pierre that Alex had courage, and that he would give him a chance to prove it?

2. The person paying Scorpia millions of pounds to destroy British-American relations hailed from China, South America, South Africa or the Middle East?

3.   What was the name of the Russian who
     owned a large property on Skeleton Key?

4.   Apart from Alex, were there eleven, twelve,
     twenty-one or twenty-seven other trainees at
     Scorpia's training centre?

5.   How many Prime Ministers had Sir Graham
     Adair worked with: four, five or six?

6.   In *Stormbreaker*, who as a schoolboy sat next
     to the boy who became Prime Minister?

7.   Who ordered Conrad to go and kill the
     Salesman?

8.   How many sisters did Felix Lester have?

9.   Who told Damian Cray that Alex had a close
     friend called Sabina?

10. Was Mrs Jones, Dr Grief, Mr Baxter or
     Mrs Stellenbosch the assistant director of
     the Point Blanc Academy?

11. What sort of weapon did Alex spot being worn
     by someone at his uncle's funeral?

12. What device was disguised as a remote
     control and used by the Chinese guard to
     trigger the water cooler at Wimbledon?

13. Was Harold Eric Lunt the real name of Alan Blunt, Damian Cray, Herod Sayle or Yassen Gregorovich?

14. Who had planted the explosives on the Mayfair Lady boat in Miami?

15. On what day of the week did Alex Rider see Blunt and Jones for the last time in *Stormbreaker*?

16. From which Middle Eastern country did Herod Sayle originally come?

17. What was the first object that Smithers gave Alex in *Skeleton Key*?

18. Did Point Blanc Academy normally have six to seven, twenty to twenty-five or ninety to one hundred pupils?

19. Who, at Ian Rider's funeral, was acting as the chairman of the Royal & General Bank?

20. Did Mrs Rothman disguise herself as a policewoman, a hospital orderly, a nun or a bag lady to get away from the SAS?

21. What is the codename given by Scorpia to their new powerful weapon that cannot be seen?

22. What colour body paint did Alex use when creating his disguise for Mrs Rothman's masked ball?

23. Who was Alex's doctor at St Dominic's Hospital: Dr Hayward, Dr Roberts, Dr Three or Dr Sing?

24. Alex and Tamara were locked in a cell with what sort of ape?

25. In *Scorpia*, for how many years had Mrs Jones been Alan Blunt's deputy?

26. Did Damian Cray receive his knighthood from the Queen in 1985, 1990, 1995 or 1999?

27. Who created a diversion so that Alex could get into Mrs Rothman's masked ball without being stopped?

28. On what device were the four terahertz dishes fitted so that they could rise into the air?

29. Who helped Alex pickpocket a ticket to the launch of the Gameslayer?

30. Who was Alex surprised to see in Damian Cray's office at the software plant along with Charlie Roper?

31. Who cut Turner free of the parcel tape when he was trapped on the Mayfair Lady boat?

32. Which character in *Stormbreaker* used to work in a circus?

33. Whose telephone did Alex pick up whilst on the boat moored in the harbour at Saint-Pierre?

34. Which woman had fallen in love with Alex's father in the past?

35. Did General Sarov say he ran eight, twelve or twenty-four miles every morning before breakfast?

36. What item along with a harpoon gun did Alex use to get to the cargo plane as it took off?

37. Neverglade was the Oxfordshire home of which villain in the Alex Rider novels?

38. How many boys were at the Point Blanc Academy apart from Alex?

39. Was the name of the Edinburgh airport security guard who stopped Alex phoning: Greg Evans, Jack Kenyon, George Prescott or Billy McDonald?

40. What was the name of Sabina Pleasure's father?

41. In what make of car did Alan Blunt arrive at Ian Rider's funeral?

42. In which country did James Sprintz's mother live?

43. What nationality was the man who attacked Alex whilst he was surfing in Cornwall?

44. What was the name of the one valley that all the slopes surrounding Point Blanc ran into: La Vallée de Fer, La Vallée de Chemin or La Vallée de Cheuvre?

45. Who did Alex throw the spear at whilst taking part in the bullfight: Yassen, Raoul or Franco?

46. How old was Yassen Gregorovich in *Eagle Strike*: twenty-four, twenty-eight, thirty-five or forty-two?

47. On what floor of the Royal & General Bank was Ian Rider's office: eleventh, fifteenth, twenty-first or twenty-third?

48. What material did Alex use to make a binding for his makeshift snowboard in *Point Blanc*?

49. Did Herod Sayle have one, three, seven or nine brothers?

50. Was it on his first, third or fifth day in Venice that Alex saw the sign of Scorpia on a boat?

QUIZ 12

1. In his youth, what item falling from a window had Herod Sayle prevented from crushing two Americans?

2. How many members of the triad trying to attack Alex existed: 1000, 3500, 8000 or 19,000?

3. A model of which England footballer was turned into an explosive gadget in *Skeleton Key*?

4. The Liebherr 154 EC-H was a helicopter, a snowmobile, a crane or an assault rifle?

5. Whose Victorian house with copper domes did Alex visit in *Stormbreaker*?

6. Which member of K Unit was afraid of parachuting: Snake, Fox or Wolf?

7. Did Kaspar, Combat Jacket, Silver Tooth or Steel Watch lead Alex out of Stamford Bridge at gunpoint?

8. In *Stormbreaker*, in whose office in London did Alex find a picture of himself on holiday in the Caribbean?

9. What colour belt had Alex achieved in his favourite martial art?

10. What is the name of the hero and main character of the Gameslayer games?

11. What was the name of Viktor Ivanov's fourteen-year-old son?

12. After studying his short files on each of the other boys at Point Blanc what one word, beginning with the letter B, did Alex write down in his notebook?

13. Who does Mrs Jones bring into Alex's hospital room to help convince him to go back to Point Blanc for an attack?

14. Whose father owned lots of diamond mines: Hugo Vries, Cassian James or Tom McMorin?

15. What item of clothing did Alex use to help start a fire on the Mayfair Lady?

16. Was La Palette a nightclub, a hotel or a café in *Eagle Strike*?

17. What weapon did Kaspar wield inside Ark Angel?

18. What colour was the casing of the Stormbreaker?

19. Mrs Rothman told Alex that after attacking London, Invisible Sword would strike again, in which American city?

20. Which sports team are the first victims of Scorpia's new weapon?

21. Who was forced to play a real-life version of one of Damian Cray's computer games?

22. Were Alex, Turner and Troy staying at the Belgrano, the Valencia, the Presidente or the Aquarius hotel on Skeleton Key?

23. The organized crime gangs called yazuka appeared in which country?

24. What substance, beginning with the letter L, was found to be released into certain water coolers to affect tennis players' performance at Wimbledon?

25. The train running down the line that Alex and Fiona were on was heading for: Manchester, London or Glasgow?

26. Was the round processor in the Stormbreaker ten per cent, fifty per cent or ninety per cent cheaper to make than regular chips?

27. What was Alex forced to do when he wore a black curving hat and a uniform sewn with thousands of pearls and sequins?

28. How many people were on board Air Force One as it reached the runway at Heathrow Airport?

29. Can you name any one of the four types of nuclear missiles launched by Damian Cray in *Eagle Strike*?

30. What was the name of the island, beginning with the letter M, on which Scorpia had its training base?

31. What item did Alex use to shape the ironing board into a snowboard?

32. Alex and Paul played which sport on board Drevin's personal jumbo jet?

33. What item did one of the quad bikers use to attack Alex with immediately after the cheese wire failed?

34. Mrs Stellenbosch ordered Alex's dinner for him in Paris. Did he get stew, pork or steak as a main course?

35. When Alex used a crane to lift the barge, did the right- or left-hand joystick move the crane hook up and down?

36. How many men came to Alex Rider's house to tell him of the death of his uncle?

37. Sir David Friend had to leave the day after Alex arrived at his house, to have lunch with the president of which country?

38. Was Fiona Friend one year younger, one year older or the same age as Alex?

39. In which month of the year did Alex go with the school trip to Venice?

40. In *Skeleton Key*, Jack Starbright offered to take Alex to visit her parents in which major American city?

41. Who was Head of Special Operations at MI6?

42. 'Winning the war against drugs' was a slogan used by the police in which Alex Rider book?

43. What animal did Alex say he would rather kiss than Fiona?

44. Which two Scandinavian countries does General Sarov say will suffer large numbers of casualties after his bomb explodes?

45. Was the first car that Alex spotted being crushed at the breaker's yard: a BMW, a Rolls-Royce, a Mondeo or a Volkswagen?

46. A dozen of what type of black flower did the Gentleman order after killing Michael Roscoe?

47. What national accent did Dr Grief have when he spoke?

48. What was agent Troy's first name?

49. What type of sweet did Mrs Jones always eat?

50. In *Eagle Strike*, who did Alex meet outside Tower Records on Piccadilly Circus?

1. At which university did Herod Sayle study economics?

2. What was the surname of the family Alex spent a holiday in Cornwall with, in *Skeleton Key*?

3. Who saved Alex from the wreck of the Mary Belle?

4. Did Alan Blunt study physics, modern languages, history or mathematics at university?

5. At Wimbledon, Alex knocked the member of the Chinese triad into a refrigerator containing what food?

6. In *Point Blanc*, which item of jewellery contained a tiny but ultra-powerful explosive?

7. Alex and Sabina were given protective clothing to wear by Yassen Gregorovich before they headed to the airport. What colour was the clothing?

8. Can you name any one of the three names Herod Sayle stated he was called when bullied at an English school?

35. Was the name of the car breaker's yard: Stryker and Sons, Stryker's of East London or J.B. Stryker?

36. Just before he went diving after Turner and Troy, Garcia gave Alex: a harpoon gun, a lucky charm, a diving computer or a knife?

37. When Alex ate toast at The Snackyard on Bayside Marketplace, what city was he in?

38. What part of his body did Jerry tell Alex to keep level when BASE jumping?

39. The Sirenuse Hotel was where Alex met and had dinner with: Alan Blunt, Dr Grief, Mrs Stellenbosch or Mrs Rothman?

0. What colour was the clothing Alex wore underneath his disguise as a pizza delivery boy?

. What type of flag was fluttering from the Royal & General Bank building?

From what sort of market stall did Alex grab a bucket to defeat the bag snatchers in Venice?

In which country was Alex when he activated the stun grenade shaped in the figure of a footballer?

9. Had the Dozmary family held the tin mine in *Stormbreaker* for five, seven, nine or eleven generations?

10. What was the first name of the hotel receptionist that Alex saw killed by Force Three: Kaspar, Conrad, Kyle or Conor?

11. Which two people that Alex Rider had met before were in the front row of the press conference for the Stormbreaker computer?

12. In whose car at the breaker's yard did Alex hide and nearly get crushed as a result?

13. Were the seven boys at Point Blanc all fourteen years of age, all fair-haired or all English?

14. What did Alex hide in when being pursued and shot at by the other members of the shooting party?

15. What part of Alex's body was first touched and hurt by the breaker's yard crane?

16. Lloyd and Ramirez were two MI6 agents guarding: Jack Starbright, Alex, the Prime Minister or Mrs Jones?

17. What was the name of Alex's vegetarian cousin, as part of his cover in *Point Blanc*?

18. Did Alex's first, third or sixth bullet destroy the Stormbreaker mouse?

19. In which British city did Alex make an attempt to escape from General Sarov?

20. After being captured on Garcia's boat, who was the first person to talk to Alex: Conrad, Turner or General Sarov?

21. In *Stormbreaker*, Alex snookered Herod Sayle behind which colour ball?

22. Did the Lear Jet carrying Alex and General Sarov stop first in the United States, Canada or Ireland?

23. In *Point Blanc*, what vehicle did Alex land on to escape the machine gunner in the valley?

24. Was Nikolei Drevin killed whilst in a helicopter, on a jet ski, in a spacecraft or in a light aircraft?

25. Who actually controlled Force Three: Damian Cray, the CIA, Alan Blunt or Nikolei Drevin?

26. Who discovered Alex the first time he s out and around part of the Sayle Enterp factory complex?

27. In *Point Blanc*, which member of the s party owned an expensive gun hand-m Abbiatico and Salvinelli?

28. What nationality was the Salesman?

29. Who was to switch on the Stormbrea computer network at the launch in th Science Museum?

30. Who did Alex follow through Londo his drugs-making laboratory on the

31. Who congratulated Alex on becom youngest person in space: Tamar a Dr Sing or Ed Shulsky?

32. Did Alex first spy Combat Jacke or Steel Watch in the football gr

33. Were the first ships Alex saw i ice-breakers, destroyers, subm battleships?

34. In which English county did have a large estate?

44. Were there six, eight, ten or twelve SAS personnel accompanying Alex on their mission to Point Blanc?

45. In what year did Dr Grief clone the children Alex had seen at Point Blanc: 1983, 1987, 1991 or 1993?

46. After being drugged, Alex woke up in an old house where he met Blunt and Mrs Jones. Was the house Georgian, Victorian, Edwardian or Elizabethan?

47. Which ancient civilization featured in the game, Feathered Serpent?

48. Did Alex have to press the front cover, the back cover or the spine of the book given him by Smithers to activate its hidden weapon?

49. Which CIA agent had been recruited at the age of just nineteen: Tom Turner, Joe Byrne or Tamara Knight?

50. Can you name either of the two characters that watched Alex climb between offices at the Royal & General Bank?

1. What symbol did the Stormbreaker have on the side of its casing?

2. Who switched room numbers at St Dominic's Hospital to fool the kidnappers?

3. What colour were the boxes Alex watched being unloaded from the submarine in *Stormbreaker*?

4. What tool did Alex grab whilst in the Ark Angel space station to use in his battle with Kaspar?

5. In *Skeleton Key*, what object did Alex strap to his leg before going diving after Troy and Turner?

6. When Mrs Stellenbosch quizzed Alex about his time at Eton, what house did Alex say he was in?

7. Which MI6 agent had spent three weeks at Herod Sayle's factory complex?

8. Who was the first person Alex hit when he fired the gun in the Science Museum?

9. In *Eagle Strike*, was Damian Cray in his forties, fifties or sixties?

10. In *Ark Angel*, which SAS operative sent Alex a get-well card from Baghdad?

11. Who stole matches from the sergeant to enable K Unit to start a fire on their survival course?

12. Did a chemical explosion rock Alex's home, the Royal & General Bank or Alex's school at the end of *Point Blanc*?

13. The sniper who shot Alex in *Scorpia* was paid £50,000, £500,000 or £5 million to kill him?

14. Who forced Wolf out of the plane when parachute training by kicking him?

15. Fistral Beach was in which English county?

16. In *Eagle Strike*, which city did Jack and Alex go to after being in Paris?

17. Ian Rider was buried close to which football club's ground?

18. Which member of MI6 lived in Melbourne House in Clerkenwell?

19. Who did Herod Sayle order to kill Alex Rider?

20. Did Alex learn that the lift to the upper floors of Point Blanc academy lay behind a giant vase, a suit of armour, a statue of a female goddess or a Van Gogh painting?

21. Can you name the CIA agent who collected Alex from the airport and took him to meet Joe Byrne in New York?

22. Who was the first girl in the Alex Rider series to suggest that Alex should kiss her?

23. In *Ark Angel*, in what city did Smithers meet Alex?

24. The president of which country was visiting Sarov on Skeleton Key?

25. Who came to get Alex out of the police station prison cell after the barge-lifting incident?

26. What was the second countryside activity Alex did with Fiona?

27. What vehicle was used to kidnap Sabina from the hospital and into hands of Damian Cray?

28. What type of soup did Alex get when dining in Paris with Mrs Stellenbosch?

29. What had Alex always thought Ian Rider's profession was?

30. A kilogram of what material was bought by General Sarov at the start of *Skeleton Key*?

31. How old was Paul Drevin: twelve, fourteen, sixteen or eighteen?

32. What was the snake-like name of the special meeting of the British Prime Minister, other senior politicians and chiefs of the police and military?

33. How much was Rufus's shotgun worth: £5000, £10,000, £15,000 or £30,000?

34. Did Alex stay five, ten, fifteen or twenty days in hospital after being hit by a sniper's bullet?

35. How many times did Alex have to press the START button on his games machine to activate the smoke bomb?

36. What nickname did James Sprintz give Mrs Stellenbosch?

37. What letter in the French elevator at Point Blanc meant basement?

38. Jack Starbright's cooking always featured recipes that took less than how many minutes to prepare?

39. Which character in *Skeleton Key* had a metal plate in his head: Joe Byrne, Conrad, General Sarov or George Prescott?

40. Damian Cray's last album had contained four anti-drugs songs. What was the album called?

41. How had Nile intended Alex to die the first time he tried to kill him?

42. Which enemy of Alex's was formerly the head of the biology department at the University of Johannesburg?

43. What colour was the box containing Sarov's nuclear bomb?

44. In *Point Blanc*, what was the name of Michael Roscoe's only son?

45. What part of her body did Fiona hurt when falling from her horse?

46. When Alex dined with Mrs Rothman in Italy, was the first course they ate spaghetti, clams, mussels or ravioli?

47. Who was Chief Executive of the Special Operations Division?

48. Who was killed first at the photographic studio in *Eagle Strike*: Marc Antonio, Robert Guppy or Jack Starbright?

49. What stewed meat was Alex served when dining with Herod Sayle?

50. In *Skeleton Key*, was Alex's hotel in Miami called the President, the Delano, the Franklin or the Seaview?

QUIZ 15

1. After the Gameslayer launch in London, to which country did Jack and Alex travel?

2. What creature in the real-life version of Feathered Serpent had been covered in a suit full of spikes and razor blades?

3. At which university did Alex's father study politics and economics?

4. What was General Sarov's first name?

5. Who threw the card used to activate Sarov's nuclear bomb away into the harbour water?

6. Did Alex leave Wimbledon after the quarter-finals, semi-finals or the finals of the competition?

7. Did the Point Blanc Academy only admit boys, only admit girls or admit both sexes?

8. In which book did Alex Rider use a snowboard to escape a building on the border between France and Switzerland?

9. What was the name of the man who had placed the bomb in the Pleasures' holiday home: Juan, Costas or Raoul?

10. According to Crawley, does the prize money at Wimbledon add up to: £4.5 million, £6.5 million or £8.5 million?

11. What nationality was the tennis player, Jamie Blitz?

12. Who was the last person to sleep in the bed used by Alex in Sayle's house?

13. In *Stormbreaker*, did Felix Lester go to St Anthony's, Brookland or Halsworthy School?

14. Which one of the following was not done
    when a drugged Alex Rider was secretly
    examined: his fingerprints taken, a mould of
    his teeth made, a small transmitter fitted into
    his armpit, a lock of hair taken?

15. Was Alex four years old, seven years old or
    under one year old when his parents died?

16. What giant creature did Alex spot in the large
    aquarium in Sayle's house?

17. In *Stormbreaker*, could the Lefort Shear exert
    a pressure of five, fifty or five hundred tonnes?

18. On what street in London was the Royal &
    General Bank located?

19. In *Point Blanc*, the SASS was the secret
    service of which country?

20. Who died immediately after Sayle's aquarium
    broke?

21. What item stopped the bullet from Alex's gun
    hitting Mrs Jones?

22. What was the first name, beginning with the
    letter R, of the leader of the young shooting
    party on Haverstock Estate?

23. Which member of Force Three did Alex attack with a medicine ball catapult: Combat Jacket, Silver Tooth or Spectacles?

24. What was Nile's one serious weakness?

25. The Church of Forgotten Saints was the site for which criminal organization's plan to terrorize London?

26. Was Alex's bike a Condor: Road Xtreme, Junior Roadracer or Racer Lite?

27. How many days before the launch were the Stormbreaker computers to be shipped out of Sayle's factory complex?

28. Who performed an aerial on their surfboard to leap onto the back of a jet ski in the book *Skeleton Key*?

29. In Roscoe Tower, a famous painting of flowers was hanging next to a lift. Was it a painting by Picasso, Monet or Van Gogh?

30. Flamingo Bay was owned by which opponent of Alex's?

31. What special quality did the ski suit given to Alex by Smithers have?

32. What type of shark attacked Alex in the water around Skeleton Key?

33. Who did Alex go horse-riding with in the book *Skeleton Key*?

34. Which member of MI6 had a voice-activated door to his office?

35. Did Alex use a karate chop, a roundhouse kick or a back kick to knock out a guard in the SAS attack on Point Blanc?

36. Were Chelsea or Stratford East winning at half time in the game Alex watched?

37. Which senior member of MI6 was present at what seemed like Alex Rider's funeral in France?

38. What was the name of the company Alex discovered a brochure about in Mrs Rothman's office during the masked ball?

39. The shaft which ran from the underwater cave into Sarov's garden was called the Devil's Chimney, the Devil's Staircase or Devil's Pipe?

40. In which American building was the case against Nikolei Drevin safely stored?

41. Did Fiona say the railway tunnel was 200m, 500m, 700m or 1000m long?

42. In *Stormbreaker*, how many minutes did it take Alex to first complete the assault course: nine, eighteen or twenty-five minutes?

43. In *Eagle Strike*, was the present Smithers sent Alex: a mountain bike, a computer games console or a pair of advanced trainers?

44. What was the one item of Alex's taken by Sarov when Alex stayed at Sarov's house?

45. What activity was Fiona doing the first time Alex met her: swimming, jogging on a treadmill or playing computer games?

46. Who surprised Alex by killing most of the members of Force Three with a gun: Paul Drevin, Tamara Knight or Magnus Payne?

47. What percentage of the money from Gameslayer sales did Cray say was going to charity?

48. At which British airport did Blunt and others witness the first use of Scorpia's new weapon?

49. When Alex first met Mrs Jones and Blunt over a meal, what meat was he served?

50. In *Stormbreaker*, what did the convoy from Sayle's factory meet up with at two a.m.?

QUIZ 16

1. In which book did the British government receive a letter ordering the American government to remove all their troops from other countries?

2. Did the pupils at Brookland School call their caretaker Bernie, Eddie, Jimmy or Broomy?

3. Which member of the shooting party decided to head home early, sickened by the wounding of animals?

4. If Alex did not give Cray the flash drive, who did Cray say he would kill?

5. What was Mrs Rothman's first name: Annie, Mary, Helen or Julia?

6. Which colour button released a smokescreen from Alex's bike?

7. Was vodka, water, red wine or brandy drugged by Sarov when he dined with the President of Russia?

8. Did Alex rip his shirt, a bed sheet or a Russian flag into strips to tie up Juan?

9. Who stopped Alex from completing the fifth zone of Feathered Serpent at the game's launch?

10. What colour were the lenses of Dr Grief's spectacles?

11. In *Scorpia*, was Alex able to hold his breath for one minute, one and a half minutes, two minutes or three minutes?

12. Damian Cray's desk had around a dozen photographs on it. What did the photographs show?

13. Whose car did Jerry Harris borrow to drive Tom and Alex to the edge of the Consanto Enterprises complex?

14. Did the SAS unit including Alex approach Point Blanc by canoe, snowmobile, paraglider or on skis?

15. What television channel did Alex switch on in his Paris hotel room in *Point Blanc*?

16. Alex Rider's father, John, had killed more than two dozen targets for Scorpia: true or false?

17. When playing Feathered Serpent, did a wall of ivy, a ladder or a pillar hide a 10,000 volt electrical charge?

18. Who said they had invented a palm organizer with a flamethrower, that they liked to call a Napalm organizer?

19. Did Alex encounter a machine called a Lefort Shear: at Sayle's factory complex, in the Royal & General Bank, at the breaker's yard or while training as a spy?

20. What alcohol from his Paris hotel room mini-bar did Alex pretend to drink to give the impression of him being a troublemaker?

21. Where did Alex throw the very expensive shotgun when out shooting with Fiona's friends?

22. Did Nile and Alex make their getaway from the Consanto complex in a Ferrari, an Alfa-Romeo or a Lamborghini sports car?

23. Did Ian Rider drive a black, red or silver car?

24. Was the car breaker's yard Alex visited in Chelsea, Vauxhall, Camden or Ealing?

25. What colour was the dog Crawley had with him when he met Alex at the football match?

26. The guards at Point Blanc seemed to all be from what country?

27. In *Scorpia*, tiny traces of which metal were found in the dead footballers' bodies?

28. Behind which London railway station did Alex find J.B. Stryker?

29. Disguised as what sort of worker did Alex gain entry to Mrs Jones's flat?

30. Who did Alex fire his mobile phone dart at in the book *Skeleton Key*?

31. What device killed Max Webber: his car, mobile phone, umbrella or tape recorder?

32. What creature came to grief in the booby-trapped cave close to General Sarov's estate in *Skeleton Key*?

33. At which airport had Alex thought about getting the cargo plane to land in *Stormbreaker*?

34. Which creature's blood had Alex covered himself with to fake his own death in the Feathered Serpent game?

35. Helen Bosworth was: a double agent for the CIA, Michael Roscoe's secretary, a girlfriend of Skoda or a field agent for MI6?

36. Which three languages did Mrs Jones tell Blunt that Alex spoke besides English?

37. Moments after Alex found the boys in the cells at Point Blanc, who found him and knocked him out?

38. In which sea was Flamingo Bay: the Mediterranean Sea, the Black Sea or the Caribbean?

39. In *Point Blanc* where was Alex taken after he was let out of the police station?

40. What Caribbean island did Alex try to reach on escaping from Flamingo Bay: Barbados, Tobago, St Lucia or Jamaica?

41. Assassination was one of the four words that Scorpia stood for. Can you name two of the remaining words?

42. In which London park had Damian Cray constructed a special dome?

43. After Alex pressed the panic button in *Point Blanc*, Mrs Jones arranged a force of SAS, MI6 field agents or British Army paratroopers to fly to Geneva?

44. Who did Alex walk back from his uncle's funeral with?

45. At the bullfight, was Alex injured by the bull on its first, second or third charge?

46. Who was kidnapped while visiting a family member at Whitchurch Hospital?

47. What item from his bike did Alex use to secure one of the doors of the drug dealers' barge?

48. Ed Shulsky wielded what weapon to destroy a boat that was chasing Alex?

49. What did Alex break using the special bubblegum in *Skeleton Key*?

50. What was the name of the terrorist group that seemed to be the sworn enemy of Nikolei Drevin?

QUIZ 17

1. Which famous British explorer discovered Skeleton Key?

2. Who arrived in a combine harvester to meet Alex in the book *Point Blanc*?

3. Which MI6 agent was exchanged for an eighteen-year-old student on Albert Bridge in London?

4. What was the name of Tom's brother, who lived in Naples?

5. Who had given Alex the magnetic clips, which he used to get into Cray's software plant: Jack Starbright, Marc Antonio or Smithers?

6. What was the surname of the man from the 'bank' where his uncle had worked who visited Alex the day he learned his uncle had died?

7. What three initials were on the briefcase given to Max Grendel as a parting gift by Scorpia?

8. Who surprised and punched Alex after he had returned to Sayle's house to collect his spy gadgets?

9. In *Point Blanc*, was Baxter killed with a shot through the forehead, a stab through the heart, many shots throughout his body or by poisoning?

10. What make of motor car did Ian Rider drive?

11. Can you recall any of the three questions Herod Sayle asked Alex when he had been caught and was handcuffed?

12. Whilst with Mrs Rothman, who did Alex call to let them know he was all right?

13. Was Alex playing football, tennis, basketball or skateboarding the first time we saw him in the book *Skeleton Key*?

14. When Alex jumped and nearly fell as he climbed between offices at the Royal & General Bank, did he grab hold of the flagpole, the flag or a stone gargoyle?

15. In which book did Alex Rider climb down
    Kerneweck Shaft?

16. When Alex returned to the boat off the coast
    of Skeleton Key, who did he find stabbed in
    the back: Alan Blunt, Garcia, Turner or Troy?

17. What electronics device had been converted
    by Smithers to enable Alex to eavesdrop on
    conversations as far as fifty metres away?

18. How did Damian Cray's people first try to kill
    Marc Antonio: by poisoning him, by strangling
    him, by trying to run him over or by putting a
    bomb in his car?

19. In *Ark Angel*, what was the name of the
    hospital where Alex was recovering from
    being hit by a sniper's bullet?

20. In *Skeleton Key*, who were Marc and Carlo
    working for: Sarov, the Salesman or the CIA?

21. Neverglade was a fourteenth century building
    in England, which had been transported from
    which other country?

22. Drevin offered Alex a thousand pounds to
    his favourite charity if Alex beat him at which
    sport?

23. What was the surname of the German woman who worked for Herod Sayle?

24. What animal code name was Alex given at the training centre in *Stormbreaker*?

25. Which of Alex's game cartridges did he use last in *Stormbreaker*: Bomber Boy, Nemesis or Space Invaders?

26. What was the name of the boat owned by the Salesman?

27. What was the first school lesson Alex attended after his uncle's funeral?

28. Alex's cover as a rich kid saw him get a piercing on what part of his body?

29. Yassen Gregorovich shot a man dead for dropping a box, for not capturing Alex or for setting off a siren?

30. Which boy was shot in the shoulder and arm on Flamingo Bay?

31. In *Scorpia*, a set of terahertz dishes were found in London: were they in Notting Hill Gate, Chelsea, Clerkenwell or Wood Green?

32. Professor Sing Joo-Chan was the flight director in which Alex Rider book?

33. What colour were Alex Rider's eyes?

34. Did Alex first meet Dr Karl Steiner on Malagosto, Madeira, Malta or the Isle of Man?

35. What was the name of the woman who came to collect Alex from the Friend home in England?

36. What was the first country activity that Fiona invited Alex out to during his stay?

37. What was the name of the Stratford East footballer who missed a penalty in the game Alex watched?

38. In which book was Alex given a waterproof mobile phone capable of firing a drugged dart?

39. Can you name either of the people Alex saw the first time he reached the second floor of Point Blanc?

40. Who carried a footstool around to enable Herod Sayle to reach the table when playing snooker?

41. What was Mrs Stellenbosch's first name?

42. When Alex made a reverse charge call using the number he had found on Yassen Gregorovich's phone, what name did the person on the other end of the line give?

43. Was the first folder Alex found in his uncle's office marked: 'Stormbreaker', 'Nerve poisons' or 'Assassinations'?

44. Who shot and killed Mrs Stellenbosch?

45. Was the name of the member of Scorpia who had been in Mossad and wore an eyepatch, Max Grendel, Dr Three or Levi Kroll?

46. When Nadia Vole pulled the arm of a statue, Alex was propelled into a prison cell, the aquarium or a locked van?

47. In *Eagle Strike*, how many black Smart Cars surrounded Alex in Amsterdam?

48. Who had left a dry suit and tied a rope to a rock in the underwater tunnel heading towards Sayle Enterprises?

49. Alex escaped from being drowned by a flood in Venice in which book?

50. Who locked Alex in the hold of the sunken transport ship in the book *Ark Angel*?

QUIZ 18

1. Did Sarov tell Alex that there were six, forty or one hundred nuclear submarines where they were heading?

2. Was Paul Drevin in hospital due to: appendicitis, heart murmurs, severe asthma or a broken leg?

3. Just outside which European city did Damian Cray have a software plant: Paris, Hamburg, Brussels or Amsterdam?

4. Who rushed out of Haverstock Hall threatening to give Alex's cover away to Mrs Stellenbosch?

5. Flying in Drevin's personal Boeing 747, did Alex and the others touch down in the United States, Canada, Barbados or Mexico?

6. Dr Rachel Stephenson was a researcher in the field of poisons, nuclear weapons, nanotechnology or industrial spying?

7. What was the name of the cartridge that turned Alex's portable games machine into a smoke bomb?

8. What was the name of the Force Three terrorist whose face was tattooed with a map of the world?

9. Was Smithers wearing a Mickey Mouse T-shirt, a Hawaiian shirt or a baseball jacket when he met Alex in *Ark Angel*?

10. At which university had Blunt and Roscoe met and become friends?

11. Was Wolf, Alex or Blunt shocked by an HRT Stun Grenade?

12. Did Alex and Fiona escape the oncoming train on foot, on horseback or using bicycles?

13. How did Alex Rider leave the cargo plane to try and warn people of the threat of the Stormbreakers?

14. Who unlocked Alex's handcuffs only to lead him into another trap in *Stormbreaker*?

15. From what country did Sir David Friend believe the name Stellenbosch came?

16. Who did Nikolei Drevin race on his go-kart track?

17. Where did Alex see Yassen Gregorovich while he was staying with Sabina's family: Saint-Michel, Saint-Pierre or Saint-Ricard?

18. In *Eagle Strike*, what colour was the suit worn by the bald, fat man called Franco?

19. Who had taught Alex Rider to drive?

20. Was Dr Hugo Grief almost forty, fifty, sixty or seventy years old?

21. What was the name of the school, beginning with the letter B, that Alex attended?

22. What was the nickname of the man Turner had to meet on his boat in Miami?

23. What was the name of the boy Alex discovered in the same cell as James Sprintz: Paul Roscoe, Hugo Vries or Tom McMorin?

24. Did Alex carry a flare pistol, a machine gun, a harpoon gun or a spear from Herod Sayle's house when trying to reach the cargo plane?

25. How many quad bikers attacked Alex while he was walking near Port Tallon?

26. In *Skeleton Key*, doctors from the Czech Republic, Russia, Iran or Albania had repaired Conrad's body after a bomb he was carrying exploded?

27. Did Alex take a cab, the tube, a bus or did he cycle to the Royal & General Bank on his first visit?

28. In *Point Blanc* who did Alex pretend to be searching for at the building site to get to the giant crane?

29. Who had planned to escape from the Point Blanc Academy one day, only to appear obedient and not want to escape the next?

30. When watching film of his father's apparent death, who did Alex spot giving the orders to fire at his father?

31. At the start of *Skeleton Key*, how many men flew into the island in a Cessna light plane?

32. What was the number of the engine that sucked Damian Cray in and killed him?

33. Whose mother had the first name Liz?

34. Roscoe Tower was in the middle of which large American city?

35. What was the name of the island that was the launch site for the Ark Angel project?

36. Was Fiona hostile, friendly or indifferent to the idea of Alex staying with her family?

37. Was the school secretary in *Stormbreaker* in her twenties, thirties, forties or fifties?

38. In *Scorpia* did an Airbus 300, a Boeing 747, a Lockheed Tristar or a Lear Jet bring the England reserve football team back to Britain?

39. Did Conrad have more than ten, twenty or thirty metal pins in his body?

40. What sort of accident did Alex tell people he suffered to explain his bullet wound?

41. In what country did Dr Grief use political prisoners for his experiments?

42. Whose office had a sofa that split in two to accommodate a lift from below?

43. What type of hand-held gaming device did Smithers give Alex?

44. What colour was the horse that Fiona rode when Alex accompanied her?

45. What item did Alex use as a blowpipe to knock out the guard outside Mrs Jones's apartment?

46. The Feathered Serpent game had how many zones?

47. Was the barge containing Skoda forty, sixty, eighty or one hundred metres above the ground when the metal stanchion broke and the barge fell?

48. What was the name of the largest waterway in Venice?

49. Who was the leader of K Unit: Wolf, Eagle or Fox?

50. Was one of the bodyguards, the President of Russia or Conrad the first to react to the drugged drinks at Sarov's dinner?

1. How many hours had Alex been given to complete the long survival hike during training in *Stormbreaker*?

2. What name had Drevin given to the Atlas rocket heading to dock with Ark Angel?

3. In *Skeleton Key*, was the man who attacked Alex at Fistral Beach killed in the attack, or was he caught and interrogated by MI6 or did he escape unharmed?

4. How many people were on the podium for the launch of the Stormbreaker computers in the Science Museum?

5. Who opened the main door to Air Force One as it was moving on the runway and about to take off?

6. In *Ark Angel*, who did Alex encounter at the equipment store when he was trying to get hold of the kite-surfing equipment to escape?

7. What object did Alex use to hit the first Chinese triad member who attacked him underneath Wimbledon?

8. What drink did Alex have with his dinner in Paris with Mrs Stellenbosch?

9. What was the name of Sir David Friend's wife?

10. How many snowmobiles pursued Alex down the mountainside away from Point Blanc?

11. Which project did Drevin tell Alex was billions of pounds over budget?

12. What was the name of the only friend of the same age Alex made in his first week at Point Blanc?

13. Did Mrs Stellenbosch drink champagne, whisky, gin or tap water when eating dinner in Paris with Alex?

14. Did Alex Rider get into Cray's software plant near Amsterdam stuck to the outside, hiding inside or hiding underneath a lorry?

15. What exploding item of jewellery had been removed from Tamara Knight after she was captured?

16. In which city were Sabina and Alex when they had a serious row: Paris, Amsterdam, New York or London?

17. *Dai-lo* means big brother, little brother or leader?

18. When Alex encountered the bomb on board Ark Angel were there fifteen, twenty-one, twenty-seven or thirty-six minutes to go before it exploded?

19. The jellyfish in Sayle's aquarium was at least two, five or ten metres long?

20. Which opponent of Alex's in *Point Blanc* tells him that they know his CD player can send a signal but not messages?

21. When Alex first turned the offer of spy work down, what sports job did he say he wanted to do instead?

22. Jerry took an altitude reading just before Alex BASE jumped. Was it just over 250m, just over 350m or just over 450m?

23. While surfing in Cornwall, Alex was attacked by a man on what sort of vehicle?

24. Was Sabina's mother a TV presenter, a journalist or a fashion designer?

25. How many pounds per point did Alex and Herod Sayle play for during their game of snooker?

26. In what month of the year was Alex staying at the Friend family estate?

27. Which one of the following was not a stuffed animal head in the reception of the Point Blanc Academy: lion, tiger, antelope, water buffalo?

28. When Alex was training as a spy, what two letters meant a rendezvous point: RP, RV or RZ?

29. Was the Thruster, The Soarer, The Cribber or The Tornado, the largest wave ever to hit the English coast?

30. What shape was the earring stud given to Alex by Smithers?

31. Who gave Ian Rider his last assignment?

32. In which English county were Damian Cray's massive house and grounds: Sussex, Somerset, Dorset or Wiltshire?

33. In which book did a scientist plan to replace sixteen children of rich people with clones that he had made?

34. In what part of London did Alex live with Ian Rider?

35. Who tells Alan Blunt that Alex has been scarred and has changed after his mission to Skeleton Key?

36. What item did Alex use to open the door of his cell at Point Blanc?

37. Alex's cover in *Point Blanc* includes him being expelled from what famous school?

38. Who lied to the Prime Minister and others saying that he had sent Alex to Venice to work undercover?

39. Was the Gentleman paid US$ 20,000, US$ 200,000 US$ 2,000,000 or US$ 20,000,000 to kill Michael Roscoe?

40. Did Alex go to Mrs Rothman's masked ball dressed as: a doctor, a Turkish slave, a pizza delivery boy or a clown?

41. What was the name of Marc Antonio's friend who collected Alex from the café: Robert Guppy, Henrik Masterson or Jacques Cloyer?

42. Can you name two of the four items Alex Rider bought from the maritime store in Port Tallon?

43. Was Alex by Trafalgar Square, Buckingham Palace, Marble Arch or Downing Street when he made a phone call to Scorpia to come and collect him?

44. Edward Pleasure was taken by helicopter to Montpellier, Grenoble, Lyons or Bordeaux?

45. Did Ark Angel weigh about 100, 300, 500 or 700 tonnes?

46. Was Michael Roscoe forty-four, fifty-four or sixty-four when he was murdered by a contract killer?

47. When Alex met him had James Sprintz been at Point Blanc for more or less time than Hugo Vries?

48. In what room in Point Blanc Academy was Alex stunned to find lots of photographs of himself?

49. Which block at Sayle Enterprises housed software development: Block B, C or D?

50. In *Eagle Strike*, did Yassen, Raoul or Franco have two gold teeth?

HARD QUESTIONS

1. What was Mrs Jones's real first name?

2. Can you recall the name of the New York gallery used as a front by the CIA?

3. At what hour was Alex Rider woken up to be told of the death of his uncle?

4. What was the name of Crawley's pet dog in *Skeleton Key*?

5. How many rooms did Alex think were contained in the Paris hotel owned by the Point Blanc Academy?

6. Who was the wife of footballer, Adam Wright, in *Ark Angel*?

7. What was the name of the band that Damian Cray formed in the seventies?

8. Which of Alex's games cartridges did he use first once he arrived at Herod Sayle's house?

9. The cargo plane found in the middle of the Cray Software Technology plant was daubed with the name of what airline?

10. Which schoolboy lived in a converted church in Hampstead?

11. What was the full name of the French terrorist group, CST, in *Eagle Strike*?

12. Which character had the middle names Charlotte Glenys and owned properties in London, New York and Tobago?

13. What title at the 'bank' did Crawley tell Alex his uncle had had?

14. Can you recall the name of the pizza company that was part of Alex's cover prepared for him by Scorpia?

15. How many dollars had Dr Grief paid Baxter for his plastic surgery work?

16. In *Eagle Strike*, V1 was decision speed for Air Force One, above which the pilot could not stop the plane from taking off without crashing. Can you recall what that speed was in miles per hour?

17. What make of car took Alex from London to Cornwall to meet Herod Sayle?

18. Sabina used to mark French boys out of twenty for looks. What mark did she give Alex?

19. What was the name of the head teacher of Brookland School?

20. Dr Karl Steiner performed an inkblot test on Alex. When others at Scorpia saw a gun pointed at the head of a person, what did Alex see?

21. What was the brand name of the mosquito repellent which was actually an insect-attracting liquid given to Alex by Smithers?

22. What was the name given to the mock-up of an embassy which was used to train Alex and K Unit?

23. In *Scorpia*, what were the names of Max Grendel's twin grandchildren?

24. What was the name of the street in Lebanon where Herod Sayle saved the lives of two rich Americans?

25. Who was recovering from serious injuries in Lister Ward in the book *Eagle Strike*?

26. When Mrs Stellenbosch quizzed Alex about his time at Eton, what word, beginning with the letter D, did Alex use to describe lessons?

27. What did Alex do with his shirt when he played the real-life version of Feathered Serpent?

28. What was the name of the Brooklands School Secretary?

29. Can you name the Aztec god in *Eagle Strike* that was half-human, half-alligator?

30. *Physalia physalis* was the Latin name of which creature in *Stormbreaker*?

31. What was the name of the hotel in Paris where Alex and Mrs Stellenbosch spent the night?

32. In *Stormbreaker*, what was the name of the public house in Port Tallon?

33. What was the name of the house Sabina's family rented in Cornwall in the summer holidays?

34. Which cartridge turned Alex's games machine into an X-ray device?

35. What was the name of the cemetery on the Fulham Road where Ian Rider was buried?

36. What was the codename of the English man who shot and killed the Commander at the start of *Eagle Strike*?

37. By what name was the contract killer who murdered Michael Roscoe known?

38. What was the name of the barge that Skoda and his friend were on?

39. How many millions of pounds was striker Adam Wright bought for by Nikolei Drevin?

40. In what sort of luxury vehicle was Alex driven to meet Sir David Friend?

41. What was the name of the drug dealer who worked with Skoda?

42. How many millions of pounds had Scorpia been offered to destroy the relations between the two countries of the United States and the United Kingdom?

43. What was the name of the Aztec god in Cray's Feathered Serpent game whose feet were facing backwards?

44. In which book was Rodriguez head of airport security?

45. What was the name of the hilltop village from which Alex found a way into the Consanto complex?

46. In *Skeleton Key*, what sound was picked up by a sensor and replayed to Alex after he hid in the limousine?

47. Who used a Russian handgun called a Grach MP-443?

48. Can you recall the title of the book with the code CL 475/19 in Port Tallon library?

49. What was the name of the removals company who cleared out Alex's uncle's room at home?

50. What was the name of the man that Alex's father had appeared to kill in a pub, receiving a four-year prison sentence as a result?

ANSWERS

EASY ANSWERS

1. British
2. Ian Rider
3. Karate
4. A computer
5. Smithers
6. MI6
7. London
8. Tom
9. Italy
10. *Stormbreaker*

11. Mrs Jones
12. *Ark Angel*
13. Strawberry
14. A goofy stance
15. Point Blanc
16. A ball boy
17. Ark Angel
18. Jack Starbright
19. The President of the United States
20. Damian Cray

21. Alex Rider
22. *Eagle Strike*
23. The third bull
24. *Skeleton Key*
25. Smithers

26. A surfboard
27. An ape
28. *Scorpia*
29. Sabina
30. Jack Starbright

31. Nikolei Drevin
32. Russia
33. Special Air Service
34. Alex Rider
35. Nile
36. The Amazon jungle
37. Mrs Stellenbosch
38. His arm
39. Mr Grin
40. Russia

41. *Skeleton Key*
42. Miss
43. A scorpion
44. London
45. True
46. *Ark Angel*
47. Skoda
48. Fourteen
49. American
50. In a plane crash

QUIZ 1

1. A journalist
2. Kolo
3. A birdwatcher
4. Ten o'clock
5. Royal & General
6. Smallpox
7. Sir David Friend and his family
8. Herod Sayle
9. Zit-Clean
10. Q

11. Televisions
12. Michael J. Roscoe
13. A nuclear bomb
14. Beer
15. False
16. Two
17. Green
18. Sugar plantation
19. James Sprintz
20. Stratford East

21. A piece of paper
22. Secondary school
23. Marc Antonio
24. His drink
25. Through the window
26. Sabina
27. Tom Harris
28. His head
29. Lots of scorpions
30. The Big Circle

31. A sword
32. A cola bottle
33. Nematocysts
34. Stamford Bridge
35. Above the screen
36. Heathrow Airport
37. A hand grenade
38. Washington
39. Venison
40. General Sarov

41. Dr Grief
42. A medallion
43. 999
44. A quarter of a million dollars
45. Consanto Enterprises
46. Chaos
47. He believed him
48. Mrs Rothman
49. Tokyo
50. Second cell

QUIZ 2

1. Mrs Stellenbosch
2. The crossbow
3. Murmansk
4. Dr Grief, Mrs Stellenbosch
5. A coke
6. Henryk
7. Six
8. Sam Green
9. Three
10. Alex Rider

11. A plastic card
12. Joe Canterbury
13. The Japanese ninjas

14. Black
15. Smithers
16. Old Street
17. MI6
18. Eight
19. Yassen Gregorovich
20. Sabina's father, Edward Pleasure

21. Force Three
22. Grenoble
23. The CIA
24. Blue
25. Ten seconds
26. Alex Rider
27. 100 mph
28. Smithers
29. True
30. San Francisco

31. Mr Grey
32. The round processor
33. 3900kg
34. John Crawley's
35. Miss Bedfordshire's
36. California
37. American
38. Michael Roscoe
39. Jerry
40. 300

41. Minister for Science
42. A finger
43. 2500
44. A laboratory
45. Number 10 Downing Street

46. The Science Museum
47. The back window
48. Fiona
49. Six buttons
50. PE teacher

QUIZ 3

1. Mr Lee
2. Ski goggles
3. Personnel Manager
4. Drugs
5. Black
6. Raoul
7. *Skeleton Key*
8. A helicopter
9. Nile
10. Whitchurch hospital

11. Skeleton Key
12. A vitamin booster
13. The Cribber
14. Dr Grief
15. Naples
16. Rufus, Max, Bartholomew, Fred, Henry
17. The yo-yo
18. The US President
19. Nikolei Drevin
20. The England reserve football team

21. English
22. A window
23. Mrs Rothman
24. Alex Friend
25. Sixteen

26. Port Tallon
27. The British government
28. Lucky
29. One
30. Breakfast

31. Manchester United
32. Mrs Jones
33. K Unit
34. Afghanistan
35. *Harry Potter and the Chamber of Secrets*
36. Paul Drevin
37. Through a railway tunnel
38. Bubbles
39. A fishing net
40. A fork-lift truck

41. Machine guns
42. Blue
43. A ski suit
44. A junior matador
45. Malta
46. Yassen Gregorovich
47. The CIA
48. The police station car park
49. Crawley
50. Scotland

QUIZ 4

1. Eighteen
2. One
3. Alex Rider
4. A ski jump
5. Pigeons
6. He wore an eye patch

7. The CD player
8. £300 million
9. Alex Rider
10. A rifle

11. General Sarov
12. Conrad
13. Elton John
14. Sayle Enterprises
15. The Taj Mahal, the Eiffel Tower, the Colosseum, the Tower of London
16. A Game Boy Advance
17. Jerry Harris
18. Murmansk
19. Max Grendel
20. Mr Donovan

21. He drove off the cliff
22. Helicopter
23. Beethoven
24. Mrs Stellenbosch
25. London
26. Her fingers
27. Magnus Payne
28. His hand
29. Spectacles
30. A crossbow

31. Nikolei Drevin's
32. Dr Hugo Grief
33. Norfolk and California
34. Damian Cray
35. Sabina
36. Drugs
37. Falling down a lift shaft
38. Jacques Lefevre

39. Thirty metres
40. True

41. Snake
42. An inhaler
43. Giant chessboard
44. Vladimir
45. Oliver d'Arc
46. Xipe Totec
47. 24 hours
48. A pair of thick glasses
49. Blackpool funfair
50. Nikolei Drevin

QUIZ 5

1. Fourteen
2. Three
3. Caviar
4. His son, Paul
5. Nadia
6. Mrs Jones
7. Two swimming pools
8. Ian Rider
9. The Pacific Ocean
10. Charlie Roper

11. Ten
12. Four
13. Jack Starbright
14. Three
15. Project Gemini
16. Five minutes
17. Beirut
18. Sir Graham Adair
19. Paul Drevin
20. Number One Court

21. An architect
22. Herod Sayle
23. A Boeing 747 (747-200B)
24. Multi-storey car parks
25. JFK Airport
26. CIA
27. Guadeloupe
28. The Military Cross
29. Gardiner
30. A bug finder

31. Crocodiles
32. Mr Grin
33. Twelve years
34. The palace of the widow
35. Conrad
36. Jack Starbright
37. Nikolei Drevin
38. Her shoe laces
39. Skeleton Key
40. Turner's

41. France
42. A circle
43. Dr Liebermann
44. Ivanov
45. Snooker, darts, table tennis
46. A bridge
47. Japanese
48. In the water around Skeleton Key
49. Damian Cray
50. Mrs Jones

QUIZ 6

1. Ian Rider
2. Alan Blunt
3. Mary Belle
4. Twelve minutes
5. A tank
6. Five
7. Unhappy
8. Yassen Gregorovich
9. March
10. Newcastle United

11. Silver Tooth
12. True
13. Hornchurch Towers
14. SELF-DESTRUCT
15. Classical music
16. The World Bank
17. Two
18. Jack Starbright
19. A snowmobile
20. Oliver D'Arc

21. Two
22. The pit with the flying creature
23. Water
24. Juan
25. Twenty-one
26. Took a shower
27. Sir David Friend
28. $2.5 million
29. The Zit-Clean tube
30. A triad

31. Four
32. Garcia

33. Ian Rider's office
34. A teeth brace
35. Twenty-five
36. A car breaker's yard
37. Tamara Knight
38. Nigeria
39. A newspaper at the airport
40. Nine

41. Mrs Stellenbosch
42. Jack Starbright
43. Dr Grief
44. Conrad's
45. His uncle's office
46. The shotgun's barrels
47. Caesium
48. Gameslayer
49. Four
50. Mr Crawley

QUIZ 7

1. Y
2. Thirteen
3. Miami
4. Damian Cray
5. Three
6. *Point Blanc*
7. Ground and first floors
8. 300-1
9. Jack Starbright
10. April

11. Bridge
12. Tom
13. Herod Sayle's
14. Reading

15. Twenty
16. 90 minutes
17. Nile
18. A Siberian tiger
19. A black widow
20. Riverview House

21. Joe Canterbury
22. Forty kilometres
23. A boat
24. The basement
25. Metal
26. Little brother
27. Cornwall
28. The Netherlands
29. The Paras
30. Three

31. Tom McCorin
32. Yassen Gregorovich
33. Canoes
34. Nile
35. Battersea Power Station
36. His knee
37. James Sprintz
38. Two
39. Colin
40. Five

41. Rue Britannia
42. Twenty million pounds
43. Blue
44. Botany
45. His tube of Zit-Clean cream
46. A woman
47. Two million pounds

48. Dr Liebermann
49. Bike pump
50. Elton John

QUIZ 8

1. *Scorpia*
2. BUBBLE-0-7
3. His stomach
4. Chelsea
5. Black
6. Charlie Grey, Miss Bedfordshire
7. An ironing board
8. Damian Cray
9. On his left arm
10. He climbed up the chimney

11. The President of Russia
12. General Sarov
13. One
14. Nemesis
15. Scorpia
16. Santiago Airport
17. A removals van
18. A guard
19. His mother
20. Sixty

21. Buckets
22. A painting
23. Conrad
24. Lizard
25. Turkey
26. Brecon Beacons
27. Sabina Pleasure

28. Fiona
29. Felix Lester
30. An agent of MI6

31. A karate move
32. France
33. Snooker
34. Viruses
35. Superglue
36. Yamaha
37. Paul
38. Use his own name
39. By hiding in the limousine boot
40. £4100

41. Nile
42. A barge
43. Five
44. Rufus
45. His tongue (he had bitten it)
46. The Harry Potter book
47. Yassen Gregorovich
48. Sir David Friend
49. Ian Rider
50. The Cubans

QUIZ 9

1. Five thousand euros
2. Four
3. His double
4. The green button
5. Belinda Troy
6. Fiona
7. Crawley
8. A flick knife

9. The school football team
10. CIA

11. Nerve gas
12. London
13. *Eagle Strike*
14. Twenty million
15. Dr Baxter
16. Red
17. Ten
18. Orange
19. Conrad
20. Combat Jacket

21. Five seconds
22. A sick note from a doctor
23. Ian Rider
24. Two
25. Moscow
26. In charge of ball boys and girls at Wimbledon
27. Chinese
28. Bullet holes
29. The computer games console (the Game Boy Advance)
30. A mountain bike

31. Chocolate milk
32. In the toilet
33. Red and white
34. A taxi cab driver
35. Thirty
36. Gin
37. Charlie Roper
38. Wolf

39. Hyde Park
40. Max Webber
41. Cyanide
42. Her shoulder
43. Block D
44. His twelfth birthday
45. Herod Sayle
46. Barcelona
47. A radiator
48. Three
49. Five and a half hours
50. Two

QUIZ 10

1. Flamingo Bay
2. Alan Blunt
3. Michael J. Roscoe
4. Three
5. Mrs Rothman
6. World War II
7. A submarine
8. Twelve
9. Four hours
10. By dissecting him alive

11. Write letters
12. Fiona Friend
13. 200,000 US dollars
14. Three times
15. The Fast Forward button
16. The flying razor boomerang
17. The head of the Metropolitan Police
18. One millimetre

19. Four
20. A skateboard
21. A spear
22. Four
23. James Sprintz
24. Cossack
25. Once a week
26. A fire poker
27. Force Three
28. Feathered Serpent
29. Red
30. A C-130 Hercules

31. A wide-screen television
32. Yassen Gregorovich
33. Naples
34. Cuba
35. Shoplifting, vandalism, possession of drugs
36. A gas leak
37. A C-130
38. Paul
39. Inside the bicycle bell
40. His foot

41. Three
42. A helicopter
43. Herod Sayle
44. Conrad
45. Laptop computers, rock music
46. Thirteen people
47. Wolf
48. Nile
49. A crossbow
50. Mrs Jones

QUIZ 11

1. Yassen Gregorovich
2. The Middle East
3. General Sarov
4. Eleven
5. Six
6. Herod Sayle
7. General Sarov
8. Two
9. Yassen Gregorovich
10. Mrs Stellenbosch

11. A gun
12. A fake mobile phone
13. Damian Cray
14. Conrad
15. Saturday
16. Lebanon
17. A mobile phone
18. Six to seven
19. Alan Blunt
20. A bag lady

21. Invisible Sword
22. Gold
23. Dr Hayward
24. An orang-utan
25. Seven
26. 1990
27. Tom
28. A hot air balloon
29. Jack Starbright
30. Yassen Gregorovich

31. Alex
32. Mr Grin
33. Yassen's

34. Mrs Rothman
35. Twenty-four miles
36. His yo-yo
37. Nikolei Drevin
38. Six
39. George Prescott
40. Edward Pleasure

41. A Rolls-Royce
42. England
43. Chinese
44. La Vallée de Fer
45. Franco
46. Thirty-five
47. Fifteenth floor
48. Part of a bed sheet
49. Nine
50. Fifth day

QUIZ 12

1. A piano
2. 19,000
3. Michael Owen
4. A crane
5. Herod Sayle's house
6. Wolf
7. Steel Watch
8. Ian Rider's office
9. A black belt
10. Omni

11. Dimitry
12. Brainwashing
13. Wolf
14. Hugo Vries
15. His shirt
16. A café

17. A knife
18. Black
19. New York
20. The England reserve football team

21. Alex Rider
22. The Valencia
23. Japan
24. Lithium
25. Glasgow
26. Ninety per cent cheaper
27. Take part in a bullfight
28. Five
29. Minutemen, Trident D5s, Poseidons, Peacekeepers
30. Malagosto

31. His special CD player
32. Table tennis
33. A flamethrower
34. Steak
35. The right-hand joystick
36. Two
37. France
38. One year older
39. September
40. Chicago

41. Mrs Jones
42. *Point Blanc*
43. The horse
44. Norway and Finland
45. A Mondeo
46. Tulips
47. South African
48. Belinda

49. Peppermints
50. Sabina

QUIZ 13

1. Cambridge
2. Pleasure
3. Tamara Knight
4. Mathematics
5. Strawberries
6. An earring
7. White
8. Herod Smell, Goat Boy, The Dwarf
9. Eleven generations
10. Conor

11. Alan Blunt, Mrs Jones
12. Ian Rider's
13. All fourteen years of age
14. A lake
15. His head
16. Mrs Jones
17. Oliver
18. The third bullet
19. Edinburgh
20. Conrad

21. The pink
22. Canada
23. A goods train
24. In a light aircraft
25. Nikolei Drevin
26. Nadia Vole
27. Rufus
28. Mexican
29. The Prime Minister
30. Skoda

31. Ed Shulsky
32. Silver Tooth
33. Ice-breakers
34. Lancashire
35. J.B. Stryker
36. A diving computer
37. Miami
38. His shoulders
39. Mrs Rothman
40. Black

41. A Union Jack
42. A flower stall
43. Scotland
44. Six
45. 1987
46. Elizabethan
47. Aztec
48. The spine
49. Tamara Knight
50. Alan Blunt and
    Mrs Jones

QUIZ 14

1. A lightning bolt
2. Alex
3. Silver
4. A hammer
5. A knife
6. The Hopgarden
7. Ian Rider
8. The Prime Minister
9. Fifties
10. Wolf

11. Alex
12. Alex's school

13. £50,000
14. Alex Rider
15. Cornwall
16. Amsterdam
17. Chelsea
18. Mrs Jones
19. Mr Grin
20. Behind a suit of armour

21. Ed Shulsky
22. Fiona Friend
23. New York
24. Russia
25. Mr Crawley
26. Horse-riding
27. An ambulance
28. Soupe de moules
    (mussel soup)
29. Banking
30. Uranium

31. Fourteen
32. Cobra
33. £30,000
34. Ten days
35. Three times
36. Mrs Stomach-bag
37. S
38. Ten minutes
39. Conrad
40. White Lines

41. By drowning
42. Dr Grief
43. Silver
44. Paul
45. Her ankle

46. Ravioli
47. Alan Blunt
48. Robert Guppy
49. Goat
50. The Delano

QUIZ 15

1. France
2. A snake
3. Oxford University
4. Alexei
5. Alex Rider
6. The quarter-finals
7. Only admitted boys
8. *Point Blanc*
9. Raoul
10. £8.5 million

11. German
12. Ian Rider
13. St Anthony's School
14. A small transmitter fitted into his armpit
15. Under one year old
16. A jellyfish
17. Five hundred tonnes
18. Liverpool Street
19. South Africa
20. Nadia Vole

21. Bulletproof glass
22. Rufus
23. Combat Jacket
24. He was scared of heights
25. Scorpia
26. Condor Junior Roadracer
27. One day

28. Alex Rider
29. Van Gogh
30. Nikolei Drevin

31. It was bulletproof
32. A great white shark
33. General Sarov
34. Smithers
35. A roundhouse kick
36. Chelsea
37. Mrs Jones
38. Consanto Enterprises
39. The Devil's Chimney
40. The Pentagon

41. 1000m long
42. Twenty-five minutes
43. A mountain bike
44. His mobile phone
45. Swimming
46. Magnus Payne
47. Twenty per cent
48. Heathrow Airport
49. Roast lamb
50. A submarine

QUIZ 16

1. *Scorpia*
2. Bernie
3. Alex
4. Sabina
5. Julia
6. The blue button
7. Vodka
8. A bed sheet
9. Damian Cray
10. Red

11. Three minutes
12. Damian Cray
13. His girlfriend's car
14. Skis
15. MTV
16. False
17. A wall of ivy
18. Smithers
19. At the breaker's yard
20. Gin

21. Into the lake
22. An Alfa-Romeo
23. A silver car
24. Vauxhall
25. White
26. Germany
27. Gold
28. Waterloo Station
29. A pizza delivery boy
30. The Salesman

31. His mobile phone
32. A shark
33. Heathrow Airport
34. The snake's blood
35. Michael Roscoe's secretary
36. French, German, Spanish
37. Mrs Stellenbosch
38. The Caribbean
39. The Royal & General Bank/M16
40. Barbados

41. Sabotage, Corruption, Intelligence

42. Hyde Park
43. SAS
44. Jack
45. Second charge
46. Sabina Pleasure
47. A padlock
48. A bazooka
49. Handcuffs
50. Force Three

QUIZ 17

1. Sir Francis Drake
2. Smithers
3. John Rider (Alex's father)
4. Jerry
5. Smithers
6. Crawley
7. M U G
8. Mr Grin
9. A shot through the forehead
10. A BMW

11. Who are you? Who sent you? How much do you know?
12. Tom
13. Playing football
14. The flag
15. *Stormbreaker*
16. Garcia
17. An iPod
18. Putting a bomb in his car
19. St Dominic's
20. The Salesman

21. Scotland
22. Go-kart racing
23. Vole
24. Cub
25. Bomber Boy
26. Mayfair Lady
27. Maths
28. His right ear
29. For dropping a box
30. Paul Drevin

31. Notting Hill Gate
32. *Ark Angel*
33. Brown
34. Malagosto
35. Mrs Stellenbosch
36. Shooting
37. Adam Wright
38. *Skeleton Key*
39. Dr Baxter, Dr Grief
40. Mr Grin

41. Eva
42. Damian Cray
43. Nerve poisons
44. Wolf
45. Levi Kroll
46. The aquarium
47. Six
48. Ian Rider
49. *Scorpia*
50. Kolo

QUIZ 18

1. One hundred submarines
2. Appendicitis
3. Amsterdam

4. Fiona Friend
5. The United States
6. Nanotechnology
7. Bomber Boy
8. Kaspar
9. A Hawaiian shirt
10. Cambridge University

11. Alex
12. On horseback
13. By parachute
14. Nadia Vole
15. South Africa
16. Alex
17. Saint-Ricard
18. White
19. Ian Rider
20. Almost sixty years old

21. Brookland School
22. The Salesman
23. Paul Roscoe
24. A harpoon gun
25. Two
26. Albania
27. He took the tube
28. His dad
29. James Sprintz
30. Mrs Jones

31. Three
32. Engine number two
33. Sabina's
34. New York
35. Flamingo Bay
36. Hostile
37. Her twenties

38. A Boeing 747
39. More than thirty
40. A bike accident

41. South Africa
42. Smithers
43. Nintendo Game Boy Color
44. Grey
45. A drinking straw
46. Five
47. Sixty metres
48. The Grand Canal
49. Wolf
50. One of the bodyguards

QUIZ 19

1. Twelve
2. Gabriel 7
3. Caught and interrogated by MI6
4. Four
5. Sabina
6. Paul Drevin
7. A gas cylinder
8. Coke
9. Caroline
10. Two

11. Ark Angel
12. James Sprintz
13. Champagne
14. Stuck to the side of the lorry
15. Her earrings
16. London
17. Big brother

18. Twenty-seven minutes
19. At least ten metres
20. Dr Grief

21. Be a footballer
22. Just over 350 metres
23. A jet ski
24. A fashion designer
25. One hundred pounds
26. April
27. Tiger
28. RV
29. The Cribber
30. Diamond-shaped

31. Mrs Jones
32. Wiltshire
33. *Point Blanc*
34. Chelsea
35. Mrs Jones
36. His earring
37. Eton
38. Alan Blunt
39. US$ 200,000
40. A Turkish slave

41. Robert Guppy
42. A torch, rope, a jersey, a box of chalk
43. Marble Arch
44. Montpellier
45. 700 tonnes
46. Fifty-four
47. Less time
48. The operating theatre
49. Block B
50. Franco

HARD ANSWERS

1. Tulip
2. Creative Ideas Animation
3. 3 a.m.
4. Barker
5. Fifteen
6. Cayenne James
7. Slam!
8. Speed Wars
9. Millennium Airlines
10. Felix Lester
11. Camargue Sans Touristes
12. Julia Rothman
13. Overseas Finance Manager
14. Perelli's Pizzas
15. One million
16. 150 miles per hour
17. A Mercedes
18. Twelve and a half
19. Henry Bray
20. Someone pumping up a football
21. Stingo
22. The Killing House
23. Hans and Rudi
24. Olive Street
25. Edward Pleasure

26. Divs
27. He set fire to it
28. Jane Bedfordshire
29. Tlaloc
30. A jellyfish (Portuguese man-o'-war)

31. Hotel du Monde
32. The Fisherman's Arms
33. Brook's Leap
34. Exocet
35. Brompton Cemetery
36. Hunter
37. The Gentleman
38. Blue Shadow
39. Twenty-four
40. A Rolls Royce Corniche

41. Mike Beckett
42. One hundred million pounds
43. Xolotl
44. *Skeleton Key*
45. Ravello
46. His own heart beat
47. Yassen Gregorovich
48. *Dozmary: the Story of Cornwall's Oldest Mine*
49. Stryker & Son
50. Ed Savitt